WILD BASKETRY

HERBERT PRESS
Bloomsbury Publishing Plc
50 Bedford Square, London, WC1B 3DP, UK
Bloomsbury Publishing Ireland Limited
29 Earlsfort Terrace, Dublin 2, D02 AY28, Ireland

BLOOMSBURY, HERBERT PRESS and the Herbert Press logo
are trademarks of Bloomsbury Publishing Plc

First published in Great Britain in 2025

Copyright © Ruby Taylor, 2025

Ruby Taylor has asserted her right under the Copyright, Designs and Patents Act, 1988, to
be identified as Author of this work

All rights reserved. No part of this publication may be: i) reproduced or transmitted in any form, electronic or mechanical, including photocopying, recording or by means of any information storage or retrieval system without prior permission in writing from the publishers; or ii) used or reproduced in any way for the training, development or operation of artificial intelligence (AI) technologies, including generative AI technologies. The rights holders expressly reserve this publication from the text and data mining exception as per Article 4(3) of the Digital Single Market Directive (EU) 2019/790

Bloomsbury Publishing Plc does not have any control over, or responsibility for, any third-party websites referred to or in this book. All internet addresses given in this book were correct at the time of going to press. The author and publisher regret any inconvenience caused if addresses have changed or sites have ceased to exist, but can accept no responsibility for any such changes

Every effort has been made to contact copyright holders of material reproduced in this book. We will rectify any omissions or errors brought to our attention.

A catalogue record for this book is available from the British Library
Library of Congress Cataloguing-in-Publication data has been applied for

ISBN: 978-1-7899-4248-4; eBook: 978-1-7899-4247-7

4 6 8 10 9 7 5 3

Designed and typeset by Tina Hobson
Printed and bound by L.E.G.O. SpA, Italy

To find out more about our authors and books visit www.bloomsbury.com and sign up for our newsletters
For product safety related questions contact productsafety@bloomsbury.com

RUBY TAYLOR

WILD BASKETRY

Making baskets and
natural cordage
from foraged plants

HERBERT PRESS

Contents

Foreword	7
Preface	9
Introduction	14
1 Why 'Wild'? Why Basketry?	17
2 Origins: Animal-made Structures	31
3 Origins: Human Archaeology of Baskets and Cordage	36
4 Basketmaking Traditions	51
5 Harvesting Materials	71
6 Projects	83
1. Bramble Basket	87
2. Willow Bark Container	103
3. Cordage (Phormium, Daffodil, Bramble, Willow)	115
4. Phormium Net Bag	141
5. Lidded Grass Basket	151
6. Reed Mace Basket	161
Foraging Wild Plants: The Law	173
Bibliography	174
Resources, Photo Credits and Permissions	175
Acknowledgements	176

FEATURED ARTISTS

Jeanne K Simmons	28
Caroline Dear	34
Chris Drury	48
Martin Hill & Philippa Jones	80

Foreword

We gather round in a sunlit circle to introduce ourselves on a small East Sussex farm. The workshop begins with a silent walk into dappled woods led by artist-maker Ruby Taylor. The quiet is a necessary (re)minder to connect more naturally through our senses, attuning to the sights and sounds and fragrances, picking up birdsong, the wind's light touch, the sound of forest debris crunching under rhythmic footfalls. This feels like a walking prayer. Learning as ceremony. To begin in gratitude and relationship feels like a salve, a rare, yet deeply-longed-for medicine that allows me to (re)member I am part of this place, not an isolated individual.

I have come halfway around the world to take three wild basketry workshops with Ruby. I could tell from her spellbinding online video that we held common ground. Ruby's practical yet relational approach to teaching, and her deep love for this world becomes evident by sustainable harvest of plants and a profound care of place. Perhaps she could teach me how to shape and weave at the intersection of thought, beauty, place and personhood and find new knowledges – both metaphorically and materially – through the ancient art of basketry? As an ecopsychologist and teacher, I longed for a more embodied way of knowing, to make-to-know, to literally make-meaning.

After a brief harvesting, we move to our fire circle and claim our spots on smooth wooden benches. Ruby expertly builds a great crackling fire, careful to include everyone's breath as part of the ritual stoking. Soon, a big pot of soup begins to heat, the kettle brews and we warm ourselves as her instruction continues. Her ethics of care for our well-being and ongoingness and her generative teaching style invite ease and openness, and instill confidence.

At the confluence of plants, place, people and, well, what feels like old power in this forest, my experience is transformative. I fall into a natural rhythm of weaving and as I shape my basket, I am in turn shaped by this process, by this vessel emerging – with my hands, heart, thoughts, and newfound skills (with much unmaking and remaking too). I feel as if I'm under a spell cast between me and the vines intertwined in an intimately wild conversation.

Ruby tells me her people were indigenous to these lands (as were mine). Drawn to south-eastern England from the farthest west coast of Canada to find this gifted teacher, in happenstance, I have found a sense of homecoming that pervades my trip, even my dreams. I realise this is no mere workshop or humble instruction, rather it is an invitation to loving the world through making-with and making kin.

To move from emergency to emergence, we're going to need new skills. Or rather new-old skills. We must reclaim what has been trampled in our rush to techno-scientific solutions and machine-made goods and learn to make our way again, together. I thank the gods that Ruby cultivated her own soul's gifts to teach a more aesthetic and respectful way to live, in counterbalance to the anaesthetics of modernity; to nurture what is life-giving.

It matters to our flourishing that we share and tell old-new stories and know the ceremonies and rituals and skills of how to stitch and knit and knot and unravel if we are to be resilient and adaptive. This gem of a book tells such stories and offers primer steps to making our way home.

As Ursula Le Guin says, 'If it is a human thing to do to put something you want, because it is useful, edible or beautiful, into a bag, or a basket, or a bit of rolled bark or leaf, or a net woven of your own hair... then I am a human being after all. Fully, freely, gladly for the first time.'

← A variety of baskets made from grass, rush and wild rose, bramble, iris and honeysuckle, willow bark, ivy, pine needles and bindweed

Working my last row, I realise that this sacred place and its creatures – fire's smoky breath, wind's voice through branches, the gaze of neighbouring sheep at the fence as our fingers moved in weaving-time rhythm, the sincere conversations held beside that fire – are all woven into this sweet receptacle to be going on with, to carry me home again, more fully myself, more gladly human.

Deep gratitude to Ruby Taylor for this trove of wild basketry. She shows us, with step-by-step practicality, how to make beauty through form and function from the livingness of the world with six diverse projects. And as you become a maker yourself with each twining row (or cordage twist), revel in the quiet joy of creating something necessary and beautiful and made-by-hand which can contain and carry the stuff of life and carry us on together, gladly.

Hilary Leighton, Professor, School of Environment and Sustainability, Royal Roads University, Canada

Preface

The marvel of a basket is in its transformation, its journey from wholeness as a living plant to fragmented strands and back to wholeness again as a basket. A basket knows the dual powers of deconstruction and creation that shape the world. Strands once separated are rewoven into a new whole. The journey of a basket is also the journey of a people.

Robin Wall Kimmerer, *Braiding Sweetgrass*

I grew up in South Oxfordshire, England, on the loamy soils of the Thames Valley and chalk hills of the Chilterns, among beech trees, bluebells and the ancient monument of the Uffington White Horse. My mother worked with textiles, grew plants and encouraged me in craft projects from a young age. My father, from a long line of local growers and farmers, grew up on a large mixed farm in the early twentieth century, so he knew ancient meadows and hayricks from then, before farming became intensified. He learnt the farmers' skills of making and fixing with whatever is to hand.

When I was born it was common to leave babies on their backs in prams outside in the garden for periods of time, so I have hazy memories of gazing at wind-rustled leaves against the sky. Then later, older, searching out ladybirds in the sun-warmed, fragrant box bushes; following ant trails on the front steps; hiding out on dusty cypress boughs in a secluded part of the garden; fascination with aconites flowering at the base of the yew hedge, bright yellow among the muted hues of a winter garden. The medieval house we lived in was made largely of local materials: an oak-framed structure with wattle and daub walls, stone floors and a roof thatched with reeds. When the wind blew in a certain direction, particles of daub drifted through gaps into my bedroom, leaving a light dusting everywhere. A barn attached to the house had a dirt floor; it was dark, dry and smelt comfortingly of reeds, earth and wood.

After graduating from art college in the late 1980s, I took off for a year to Southeast Asia. One of the places we visited was the Mentawai island of Siberut in Indonesia, enticed by the entry in our travel guide which more or less said that hardly any travellers went there. We lived for a week with a clan group, deep in the jungle in their longhouse, several hours' journey by canoe and foot from the coastal resettlement project. We slept directly on the bamboo floor, ate sago (starch from the trunk of palm trees) cooked in leaves on the fire, and were accompanied by a friend of the clan group, Antonias, who translated for us. One day, we were invited to join a trip to gather green mangoes and one of the young men led us to a particular tree, deeper in the jungle. We realised he'd taken us on a long detour and later learnt this was to allow the rest of the group time to arrive ahead of us and sing their pre-harvesting song to the tree while we were out of earshot; it was a sacred song they were protective of. We learnt that a song was sung before any plant or animal was harvested from the jungle for food, clothing or building materials; all were understood to be animate. At that time, the clan group relied largely on the jungle for their needs.

We learnt that a song was sung before any plant or animal was harvested from the jungle for food, clothing or building materials; all were understood to be animate

On our final morning I woke pre-dawn to the shadowy sight of an elder in the doorway of the longhouse, silhouetted by early light, holding up a forest fowl and singing to it before taking the bird's life to feed his family. I remember the impact of that, how his rough, deep voice resonated, how profound and mysterious it felt. What reverence, what an acknowledgement of interconnectedness and the reality of taking, receiving, reciprocating. It cast a light on my own culture's relationship with the natural world where I saw greed and hubris, destruction and disrespect for gain and profit; I came from a culture with teachings about humans having dominion over the natural world. In that brief stay with the clan group I glimpsed another way, where humans' relationship to the natural world was one of sacredness and belonging, with people as an integral – not a dominant – part of the ecosystem.

In my late twenties, having trained and worked as a secondary school teacher of art and design and spent time living and working in Eastern Africa and Sri Lanka, life took unexpected turns. Within the space of a few years, more or less all the constructs of my life had crumbled or fallen away: health, marriage, relationships, home, work. I sought refuge for a year in the verdant hills, valleys and fields of Devon. It was there – in the silence and stillness of long months in a land-based Buddhist retreat community – that I recognised the value of a deeper connection to the natural world as a way to find solace, make sense of my life and give it meaning. I read Mary Oliver's poem 'Wild Geese', and realised I was searching for what she describes as my 'place in the family of things'. In fact, it felt as if my survival depended on it.

In the enfolding landscape of Devon I began to learn about relinquishment, away from daily life, dwelling in the natural time and rhythms of seasonality. With the long periods of solitude and silence of repeated retreats there, I learnt to be still like the trees in the quiet wood, walk barefoot on the flanks of the earth, let the wind blow through my hair, relish the rain on my face. A friend showed me cordage he'd made from brain-tanned deer hide; it amazed me. I became more intimately acquainted with small woodland birds and buzzards, nocturnal screams of foxes, tall trees on the hill, the waxing moon behind bare ash branches. I began to sense the sacred in it all. At moments, I felt part of the weave and that I had a place within it: being neither foreground (in the way we humans often behave) nor less important. It later became clear that this period had been a turning point for healing from the serious ill health that lasted more than a decade; a decade of living without assurance of recovery.

Throughout my formal art education I'd felt somewhat aimless. All I was sure of in my practice was that I relished working three-dimensionally in a materials-led way, but I couldn't find myself in either the paradigm of fine art sculpture or of craft. I began making assemblages from found natural materials gathered on my wanderings. Each piece embodied a sense of the place, the plants and creatures there, the weather, my state of mind at the time. Many of them I left in the landscape where I made them. Through art psychotherapy I rediscovered natural playfulness and breadth of expression. I made installations in the landscape for groups of people to connect ceremonially with the cycles of life and made artefacts to sell at craft outlets.

The year I joined East Sussex Archaeology and Museums Partnership (ESAMP) – a team that did experimental

→ Cutting bramble in late spring

archaeology and taught ancient crafts and technology – was the year I first tried basketry. My friend Anna asked me to join her for a day of weaving in the village hall, and because I wanted to spend time with her, I agreed. I was initially ambivalent about the basketmaking. I carried the cultural prejudice of it being a somewhat dusty, outdated craft. But with the insights I was gaining from the archaeology team, basketmaking caught me, and I went on to pursue formal training at City Lit in London and with numerous basketmakers. Alongside the training were personal explorations of working with wild plants and researching ancient baskets. I came to basketry as an artist, with the values of making work of heart, integrity and expression above technical precision. Fifteen years on, I'm still striving for precision in the baskets I make. There's a technical excellence that comes only from many, many repetitions of weaving the same material – for those makers, I have great respect.

At ESAMP I learnt how our ancient ancestors would have foraged all their material resources from the land around them. Through experimental archaeology I learnt how to process these raw materials for pottery, metallurgy, buildings, textiles, basketry, boat-making, hide-working, wild food and toolmaking. Basketmaking and cordage technology wove through many of these crafts and took on a new significance in my mind; I became fascinated. We constructed prehistoric-style human dwellings that started as giant upside-down basket forms with local hazel and ash poles to form the main structure, we interwove hazel rods to create the walls and roof and thatched it all with reeds that would have grown locally. Naturally, biodegradable crafts like this chimed with my increasing ecological concern for not wanting to add more stuff to the world. We shared our knowledge of ancient crafts and technologies with archaeology students, young people and the community. I met children who didn't know how to tie two pieces of string together; I began to wonder about the humanness of making, the origins of it and of the earliest baskets.

I also recognised a parallel process of learning about the evolution of ancient human crafts from the remote past, with the rebuilding of my own life from the ground up as I gradually regained my health and grew a life that felt more congruent.

Gradually all these strands wove together, taking root in my life and creative practice: in my sculptural work and also as an educator offering woodland craft courses that include the whole cycle of harvest and creating. Coming together around the fire – making alongside each other – is a timeless, convivial way of being. It's our human birthright, a natural human expression that inspires gratitude and giving back, among our ecological relations; a rich blend of ancestral memory, connection and embodied expression.

← Cutting bramble in winter

I came to basketry as an artist, with the values of making work of heart, integrity and expression above technical precision

Introduction

Making with our hands is fundamental to being human. It's a universal human activity to manipulate fibres – be they from animals or plants – to make baskets, bags and all sorts of other crafted artefacts. The focus of this book is creating with plant fibres. If you consider your own surroundings and imagine replacing all the plastic objects with items made from natural materials, you begin to get a sense of the ubiquity of basketry and natural cordage (string).

Interested in origins, I look at the possible beginnings of basketry and cordage, considering animal-made structures and the earliest archaeological evidence of human basketmaking and fibre technology from the Upper Palaeolithic records. Making with our hands combines so many areas of our thinking and doing; it's a significant aspect of what it is to be human.

Wild plants are the historic basis of established traditions of basketmaking throughout the world. There's great appeal to sourcing craft materials direct from the natural world in the place we live, as a way of having a lower carbon footprint and fully knowing the provenance of the material we're working with. This cultivates connection with the natural world and the feeling of belonging to place – basic human needs. Harvesting sustainably from our locality so that the plants we rely on – and the creatures who rely on them – can continue in their beautiful diversity is perhaps more pressing an issue than ever. As Robin Wall Kimmerer says, 'A place becomes a home when it sustains you, when it feeds you in body as well as spirit.'

The six projects for making baskets and cordage covered in this book are focused on wild plants that grow plentifully in temperate regions of the Northern Hemisphere, with information about where, how and when to harvest and process them. A range of basketmaking techniques is covered, with guidance on which other plants would be suitable, so that you can develop and further explore the skills you'll learn, with plants growing locally to you.

Woven through the book is a personal selection of international artists who make their sculptural work in direct relationship with the land, with place-specific plant materials. Their methods and approaches in these featured works have origins in basketry and plant fibre technology. Some are ephemeral, some are living forms… all are mutable in response to natural forces. They are works that tread lightly and inspire through their expression, sensitivity and reflection of our place in the landscape as humans.

My hope in writing this book is to communicate wonder and respect for plants, for the living world and for our innate human creativity.

Making with our hands combines so many areas of our thinking and doing; it's a significant aspect of what it is to be human

CHAPTER 1

Why 'Wild'? Why Basketry?

Plants and Place

What does it mean to have an intimate connection to the plants, the seasons and the land where we find ourselves? There is an embodied process in harvesting and using foraged materials for basketry; a rhythm and relationship inherent in the physical act of making; a dialogue between hands and materials.

Wild plants are indigenous or naturalised species that are naturally occurring, which is to say species that are not cultivated. They're often referred to as weeds. The origins of all basketmaking are 'wild' in the sense that the earliest baskets were made by people exploring local plants and experimenting with ways to bind and join them into a useful object or vessel. This becomes a profound indigenous knowledge of the characteristics of the plant, its life cycle, habitat and ecology. Regional traditions consequently emerge, with techniques that match the characteristics of plants in that specific bioregion. We look at this in more detail in Chapter 4.

A desire to connect to the natural world – to local place and ecosystem, including our gardens and allotments – seems more pressing in our largely digitalised lives, and is widely recognised as key to well-being. Sourcing craft materials direct from the natural world brings more appreciation for their true value. We develop an understanding of the time and energy a harvest requires; the impact of harvesting on the plants' future growth, and the impact on the complex ecosystem in which the plants grow; and the creatures dependent on those plants. The natural response of a caretaking and reciprocal relationship evolves, and with it an inevitable sense of belonging. This can sensitise us to our potential as a keystone species, meaning our capacity to engage in ways that have a beneficial impact on the overall ecology through stewardship. In the face of ecological pressures, when we're considering our carbon footprint, harvesting like this contributes to basketmaking being a satisfyingly circular soil-to-soil material culture. As Andy Goldsworthy says, 'Our lives and what we do affect Nature so closely that we cannot separate from it.'

Place also evokes belonging in terms of the cultural identity of those who gather particular plants for basketry; the baskets then carry and tell the story of that belonging. Access to materials can be affected by privatisation of land, climate change and land being turned over to developers. Baskets are artefacts that indicate social change on many levels, and the historical circumstances of a place are an intrinsic part of the narrative.

Sourcing craft materials direct from the natural world brings more appreciation for their true value

Cutting wild grass →

Making Baskets

Memory is enfolded into an object, when we handle the material to make it. Touch of the hand, essence and smell of the material intertwine. The memory of making is embedded within the skill, the knowledge of the material is encoded within the making.

Caroline Dear,
The Material Culture of Basketry

All over the world people weave, loop, knot, coil, twine, plait and join plant fibres using grasses, cane, rushes, reeds, flax, vines, leaves, bark, bamboo and wood. From these they make baskets, bags, nets, traps, human dwellings, mats, boats, woven textiles, hats, footwear, grain stores, furniture, tea strainers, animal tethers, coffins, cradles, bee skeps and a myriad other crafted artefacts.

Basketmaking is an ancient part of what it means to be human, all the more relevant now as a counterpoint to the cultural pull of a digitalised and disconnected way of living. Objects matter to us as humans: we are meaning makers, and objects are forms that generate meaning. Baskets as objects are part of a local cultural history: they reveal information about traditions, rituals, aspirations and experiences. They are containers, not only of things but of language and dialect, attentiveness and memory.

The making of basketry is a complex, haptic activity. There's a rhythmical dexterity of hands with materials that produces structural patterns to create a form. Depending on the scale and characteristics of the material, the whole body can be involved, along with considerable physical effort. The hands work together at every step, a dexterity enabled by our opposable thumbs. The maker's fine-tuned senses perceive the qualities of the material: its water content, suppleness, roughness, elasticity, resistance and variations in thickness. This is all crucial ongoing feedback and information that evolves into a dialogue between the material and the maker's hands.

↓ Wild grass and split bramble baskets

WHY 'WILD'? WHY BASKETRY?

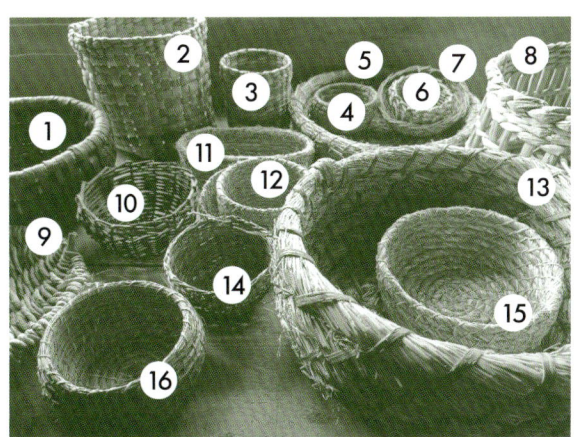

↓ Wild baskets: willow bark (1), reed mace (2, 3), wild grass (4, 5, 11, 12, 13, 15), bramble (6, 10), ivy (7), English rush (8), rush and wild rose (9), bindweed (14), pine needles (16)

Basketmaking is commonly understood to have therapeutic benefits. In Britain, after World War I, it was offered widely in occupational therapy as part of the rehabilitation of returning, wounded and traumatised servicemen. There has been study and analysis of the many facets involved in the act of basketmaking in terms of its therapeutic application. It's an activity that develops sensory-motor, visual-spatial and cognitive skills. It's also recognised as a constructive and socialising activity and can play a valuable role in relation to cases of dementia and as part of brain injury rehabilitation. In *The Material Culture of Basketry*, edited by Stephanie Bunn and Victoria Mitchell, the section 'Healing and Recovery' discusses this whole area of study in some detail.

Even when basketmaking isn't being undertaken for therapeutic reasons, once you have some experience and skill, the repetitive nature of the making can take on a meditative quality. Because basketmaking involves continuous decision-making, it requires intense concentration and is fully absorbing. This can allow the maker to slip into a flow state, which has been shown to contribute to well-being.

Sometimes basketmaking is perceived as having a lower status than other crafts, yet the skills required are of a great complexity. It takes time and practice to develop proficiency. Historically, to become a proficient maker would have involved a three- to five-year apprenticeship. A lot of skills must become embodied and integrated, gaining a familiarity with materials and techniques through repeated making over time. By making multiples of the same basket, the speed and skill of making increase greatly, as does the ability to see the level of skill expressed in a finished basket.

It's an often-quoted fact that baskets can't be made by machines. This is partly because it would probably be uneconomical to develop such a machine when there are already so many easier, cheaper ways to manufacture containers. And although you could make a three-dimensional print of a basket, the result is quite a different thing; it's not held together by the structural or material forces and techniques of a handmade basket. When you're making a basket by hand you're working in two and three dimensions simultaneously, constructing the fabric as well as the form. Since many plant materials are by their nature variable and uneven, the maker is making frequent adjustments, embodying mathematical thinking and problem-solving. Stephanie Bunn describes this as 'a bodily understanding of geometric relationships and dynamic forces, a non-verbal expression of a mathematician's or an engineer's understanding of balance, space and stresses'.

In post-industrial societies where hand-manufacturing is no longer commonplace there's a resurgence of interest in basketmaking, a renewed appreciation of the handmade, and with it a realisation of the potential loss of heritage skills. Many people's daily lives are dominated by screen time, experiencing the world digitally with a paucity of the tangible and elemental. The innate human need for the haptic cannot be denied, it seems. Tim Ingold says of the resurgence of interest in basketmaking that it isn't about slowing down or simplifying 'but it is to restore life and feeling to a world in which both are vulnerable to algorithmic decomposition'. Basketmaking is an act of defiance, then; a stand for the continued relevance of humans in the face of the digital age, in the face of artificial intelligence.

Making together and learning in person brings a certain sense of the timeless, of humans having always gathered in shared manual activity engrossed side by side. Once you feel relaxed with the process and technique there's an easy ebb and flow of speaking and silence.

→ (Top)
Splitting bramble

→ (Bottom)
Weaving bramble

This experience touches us deeply and it's often commented on by people who come to learn with me in the woods, where we sit in a circle on simple wooden benches around a small fire under the tree canopy, with not too many trappings of the twenty-first century. It's a kind of balm of togetherness, commonality, belonging in a group of humans with a common shared purpose, eating together from a single pot of food cooked over the fire as we weave the plants we foraged communally.

Making is like breathing to me – it's essential. When I'm creating with my hands – feeling and sensing the materials I've gathered in close connection to the land, plants and creatures, leaving as small a footprint as possible – life makes sense. As someone with an impatient streak, it teaches me that it just takes the time it takes, what the hands physically can do. Of course, the speed of making changes with experience, but there's still a restfulness in that; the mind and the heart can rest.

↓ Wild plants in the studio (left to right): iris, dandelion, reed mace

WHY 'WILD'? WHY BASKETRY?

↓ Wild baskets: oak (1), bramble (2, 7, 8, 10, 11),
hazel and chestnut (3), hazel (4), cedar root and wild rose (5),
English rush and wild rose (7), wild grass (9), ivy (12)

Basket
by Kay Syrad

notice the path the cool air the leaves the birds
come to the fire the flint the dark the sparking grasses
come to the way of the fire
and the quiet of the fire and wait
now here are the rushes wet-wrapped in hessian
give me the rushes the rushes
and here is the wild rose hoop shaped across knees
the rose ribs two and four tied together in arcs
in arches give me the rushes
the rushes
choose your stems hollow and round wash them down
wash them down with this simple rag
wash the rushes dark at the base
sit on the bench balance the hoop on your thighs
lift the ribs to the hoop take your rushes and weave
take your rushes and twist and weave
loop round and down and up and across
a loop a cross
and twist and weave over and under
and round and under and over and up take these rushes
wet the rushes cover the rushes
twist and weave ease a new stem in weave and wrap
measure new ribs and cut tuck into the weave
of the rushes
into the rushes the rushes
keep the space of the ribs with string and weave
in time and twist take the eye-tool to thread
tie back and trim
and love the rushes
love the rushes and the rose

← Weaving a rush and wild rose basket

FEATURED ARTIST

Jeanne K Simmons

While walking through my favourite field one autumn day, I discovered a westerly facing knoll that received the most amazing early evening light. I became captivated by this place and began visiting it often. One day in particular, I was feeling especially grateful for my intimate connection with this field and knoll, and felt a profound desire to describe this connection through my work. I suppose when we feel intense love for something, we naturally want to express it, and that was the feeling I had that day.

Having had very long hair my whole life, the idea of a braided connection to the landscape made sense to me in that moment, and shortly thereafter, I made the piece. *Extensions* involves the merging of my model's hair with the hillside, by means of a grass braid.

This piece, like the rest of my work, grew out of a desire to express my deeply held belief that we humans are an extension of the natural world, and similarly, that the natural world is an extension of us. I am preoccupied by the desire to express this belief in as many ways as I can, because it seems to me that those of us who inhabit the industrialised world have mostly lost track of this primordial dynamic. At a time when sitting on the ground can be perceived as something of a radical act, I enjoy offering images of women peacefully integrated into natural settings, usually enveloped by foraged materials that I have organised in some way.

This work addresses my concerns regarding our fragile rapport with the natural world. What I am hoping to offer the viewer is the belief that they can have a restorative experience in nature; they can sit comfortably upon the earth and become part of it, if only for a moment; they can almost step into the model and have the experience that she is having, the experience that I so often have when I am in nature. Mostly, I am hoping to rekindle and reawaken a yearning in others to connect with the natural world and to believe that we are part of the very fabric of nature.

← *Extensions*, 2020

Jeanne K Simmons grew up in coastal New Hampshire and eventually found her forever home in the Pacific Northwest of the United States, surrounded by the Salish Sea, the Puget Sound and forests of cedar, fir, moss and fern. She lives with her husband, who is also an artist. Together they raised two beautiful kids who grew up drawing pictures, making things and exploring the world around them. Jeanne has adventures in wild places every day, led and inspired by her two dogs.

jeanneksimmons.com

CHAPTER 2

Origins: Animal-made Structures

← Dunnock nest discovered in autumn; a long-abandoned nest from the previous spring. It is illegal to disturb nesting birds

In thinking about the possible origins of basketmaking, and imagining what the earliest humans might have made and with what materials, reflecting on animal-made structures seems a useful starting point. These show us how the behaviour of making and building is evident in all animals, including ourselves, with the same physical laws applying to all of us as builders. How animals build provides a biological context for our craft skills and behaviours of making baskets, and possibly points to what may have inspired the first human-made baskets.

It seems reasonable to begin by looking to our nearest living relatives: chimpanzees. Adult chimps make nests to spend the night in; they break and bend branches to create a platform which they then line with leafier branches. This kind of nest building is a feature of all living great ape species: chimpanzees, bonobos, gorillas, orangutans. Seven million years ago, around the time of our separation from our chimpanzee lineage, our ancestors were manipulating branches to make quite sophisticated nests that demonstrated an understanding of the properties of the materials.

It's worth also considering many other animals: birds and beavers build homes, wasps and termites build nests, spiders build webs to catch prey and shelters and cocoons for their eggs. The nest building of many birds and rodents far transcends anything that apes have accomplished in terms of complexity. As well as generally requiring some aspect of weaving to provide the structural integrity, they typically also include the identification and harvesting of suitable raw materials.

In the light of this, we could say that basketry is a natural phenomenon.

We and other builders use all sorts of collected materials from our environment: plant materials such as leaves, sticks, bark and roots; animal materials such as feathers, hair and sinew; and mineral materials like sand grains and mud. Weaver birds tear leaf strips to loop, weave and knot together, as do human basketmakers. Wasps turn wood fibres into pulp; we humans turn wood pulp into paper.

In his book *Built by Animals*, Mike Hansell describes the extraordinary portable home built by Difflugia corona, an amoeba (a single-cell animal with no brain). It makes its home out of hundreds of tiny grains of sand cemented together, resulting in a quite complex structure one-thousandth of a millimetre across – very much smaller than this full stop. The fact that a simple organism can make a complex structure leads to the assumption that it's genetically determined. This is because without a brain it has no capacity to learn by experience, so the instructions for making its home are recognised as being in its genes alone.

Red-tailed mason bees lay their eggs inside an empty snail shell and then plug the opening with pieces of chewed-up leaves, soil and shell fragments. The females then collect grass stalks to place in a mound on top of the shell. This is thought to protect their eggs from predators and parasites. They also chew up leaf fragments and plaster them to the outside of the same snail shell, adding to the camouflage provided by the mound of grass stems piled on top.

→ Wild baskets and netted bags

↓ Wren nest discovered in winter during the renovation of an Iron Age roundhouse reconstruction. The nest had been built in the rafters and had housed a healthy brood the previous summer

As builders, we do the best we can by working with the properties of the materials we find. So too does the weaver bird. It can make its nest from grasses because the grass has long parallel fibres; it makes a short incision with its beak in one end of the grass, and as it flies away holding the cut end, it creates a long strip of useful material. The bird knows that to make the leaf strips hold together to form a nest it must loop, weave and knot the grasses to twigs, branches and other leaves, and that only fresh, green grasses are flexible enough to do this. When the grass is dried it's too brittle to be workable. It has been identified that weaver birds use up to eight different knots including bowlines… all of this with just a beak.

In 'Bird Nest Building' in *The Material Culture of Basketry*, researchers Susan D Healey and Maria C Tello-Ramos describe the increasing evidence that birds learn from each other, as well as from their own building experience, and their nest building also depends on the environment in which they build. Male bowerbirds in Australia and Papua New Guinea build stick and grass bowers, which they decorate with all kinds of objects, such as shells, berries and stones, in order to attract females to mate with them. These display structures are unusual as they are decorative only, unlike nests built to contain and protect eggs.

This brief exploration of building structures gives, I hope, an insight into just how innate an animal activity it is to make and create. As human animals we are part of that continuum. Humans have been creative for a very, very long time: we have evidence of more than a million years of this in the form of large numbers of hand axes dating from around 1.4 million to 75,000 years ago. By 400,000 years ago, stone objects were being fashioned with great skill and sensitivity to materials, apparently as a form of art. But what about the earliest evidence of actual basketry?

FEATURED ARTIST

Caroline Dear

The Cupar Coat of Good Luck – to give its full title – was made for the Cupar Arts Festival, whose theme in 2013 was 'fate'. The Cupar burgh arms, on display at the town hall, shows three wreaths of bog myrtle, which reputedly relate to a battle in 1559 at Cupar Muir, a low hill close to the town of Cupar, where bog myrtle grew. The coat was on display throughout the festival in the window of a small clothes shop in the high street. People were encouraged to come into the shop, try the coat on, walk around the town wearing it, reflect on fate and good luck, and then bring the coat back. It had its own Facebook page (no longer existing), which showed the process of making of the coat, bog myrtle uses, and stories and images of people wearing it around Cupar. I knew the coat was working when a friend sent me a photo of someone wearing it while buying a lottery ticket.

Bog myrtle (Myrica gale in Latin, Roid in Gaelic) is a plant that grows in wet, boggy ground. In the Highlands

← *The Cupar Coat, 2013*

of Scotland, it was used for keeping midges and other bugs at bay. It's a fragrant plant with a distinctive aroma and was used in brewing beer. I made the coat using bog myrtle from close to my home on Skye, as there is none around Cupar any longer. For the body of the coat I used the green-leaved summer bog myrtle with a fringe at the bottom of red winter bog myrtle. The construction technique for the coat body is the ancient one of twining, where the vertical bog myrtle stems are held in place by overlapping horizontal ropes made from purple moor grass, which grows beside the bog myrtle.

I was delighted when a local teacher, who had seen the coat in the shop window, contacted me about having it in the school as part of a project they were doing about Ötzi the Iceman. Ötzi – dated to 5,000 years ago – was found in ice in Northern Italy and had a cloak made from twined grasses, the same technique I used for the Cupar Coat.

The heavy and fragrant coat was meant to give the wearer a moment to reflect on life, on fate, and on good luck and what this is. Being closely surrounded by a plant material for a short while, within the context of the town, was also intended to give people a moment to step outside their regular daily living, to breathe sweet-scented bog myrtle.

Caroline studied botany in Dublin before qualifying as an architect. She worked as an architect and landscape architect in Dublin, Utrecht, Oslo, London and Paris, before moving to the Isle of Skye to work in 1986. She has developed her artistic practice since then, receiving awards from Creative Scotland, Royal Scottish Academy and Hi-arts; undertaking invited residencies in Finland, Norway, Scotland and Canada; working with artistic commissions including for Alec Finlay, Hanna Tuulikki, ATLAS arts and Timespan; and exhibiting work in Canada, Norway, Finland, Scotland, Wales and England.

carolinedear.co.uk

CHAPTER 3

Origins: Human Archaeology of Baskets and Cordage

ORIGINS: HUMAN ARCHAEOLOGY OF BASKETS AND CORDAGE

Whether early humans were inspired by other animals, or whether it's a universally innate impulse to make, construct and innovate, what is the earliest evidence we have of human-made baskets and cordage, and what can this tell us about the evolution of these crafts?

Until recently, fibre technologies such as basketmaking were thought to be a relatively recent human innovation. However, although there's not a great deal of archaeological research on the use of plant fibres prior to the Holocene (i.e. before the last Ice Age, which ended 11,700 years ago), from what we do have it appears that fibre technologies, including basketry, were in fact complex and highly developed in the remote past. In some areas of Upper Palaeolithic Eurasia, for example, we have evidence of advanced basketry and loom-woven textiles dating back 30,000 years or more, with rope and twine production as early as 50,000 years ago. We don't know which came first, baskets or cordage, but currently the evidence for cordage is older.

To the contemporary basketmaker, one of the appeals of making baskets from only plant materials is that they eventually return to the earth as they biodegrade, leaving no trace: a circular soil-to-soil process. However, this same valued attribute becomes the limiting factor for learning about baskets and fibre items from the distant past, since their biodegradability means there are relatively few remains. They survive only in anaerobic conditions, closed off from microbial activity, such as in permafrost, waterlogged sites and very arid locations. What we have are glimpses and we piece together the fragments to gain an understanding, always with the possibility of other evidence existing undiscovered.

This lack of consistent evidence of datable organic materials from the remote past has hampered discussions about the order in which different crafts and technologies have made their appearance in human history. The focus has been on the best preserved and most widespread evidence: durable substances such as stone, bronze and iron. These have been used as our cultural markers, and consequently there is no 'Fibre Age'. This may arguably be a limited way of understanding our historical material culture.

The oldest-known evidence of string is an archaeological find of tiny fibres in a French Neanderthal cave, dated as 50,000 years old. These bast (inner bark) fibres – thought to be coniferous – appear to be twisted and corded, possibly three-ply. Prior to this discovery, twisted flax fibres – some of them dyed – were discovered in the Dzudzuana Cave, Georgia, dated to 34,000 years ago.

One of the appeals of making baskets from only plant materials is that they eventually return to the earth as they biodegrade

Wild Basketry

In 2016 an interesting discovery was made in Hohle Fels, Germany, dated at 35,000–40,000 years old: a perforated baton made of mammoth tusk, with traces of plant fibre found in the holes. It's thought to be a tool for making four-ply rope, produced by four or five people working together. There are precisely carved spiral grooves in the four holes, but two of those spiral clockwise and two anticlockwise, which casts some doubt on the tool's use for twisting cordage, since you'd expect the spirals to be going in the same direction as each other. Still, it's very intriguing. On page 118, I discuss cordage twist directions in more detail.

In 1993, Olga Soffer and colleagues were working with ceramic fragments dating to approximately 28,000 years ago found at Pavlov and Dolní Věstonice Upper Palaeolithic sites in Moravia (Czech Republic). They discovered impressions of patterns on the clay pieces and identified 36 different imprints recognisable as examples of textiles and basketry. The shaped pieces of clay likely came into contact with these materials while still wet, perhaps by touching the potter's clothes or being placed in a basket or on a mat. These clay fragments are too small to identify the types of objects that made the impressions, but they point to cordage, netting, plaiting of baskets, twining and loom weaving. Pollen profiles recovered from these sites indicate suitable plant species that would have been available at that time, including nettle and milkweed, alongside alder and yew. Indicating highly diverse and sophisticated textile technologies, these clay fragments are the oldest concrete evidence of the use of plant fibres for basketmaking and textiles. It's also interesting that all these same techniques are still practised today in many, many parts of the world.

→ Cutting wild grass in summer

This early evidence for ancient weaving suggests the technology was not in its infancy; it seems likely that its origins are considerably older – already an established tradition – to appear so fully formed in the Upper Palaeolithic. This shows how limited our knowledge can be when we only have stones and bones to work with, and how much is potentially missing from the archaeological record because of the fast decay rates of perishable materials like plants.

There is other archaeological evidence to consider which gives valuable insights, including bone needles, beads and carved figurines. During the Gravettian period (in Western and Central Europe and Russia, roughly 28,000–22,000 years ago), bone needles became common, useful for netting and stitching. The very small size of some of the bone needles suggests they may not have been useful for leather work, but were possibly more useful for plant fibre crafts.

Beads of shell, tooth and bone turn up with increasingly small holes during the Gravettian, with evidence (from burial finds) of them being attached to clothing and headgear in small rows. This tells us there was knowledge of sewing, and although beads themselves don't necessarily signify cordage-making, there is evidence that at least some of the thread in use at the time was twisted together from small natural fibres rather than cut from long, stringy body parts like gut or sinew. This evidence comes in the form of a carved ivory female figure wearing a string skirt: the Lespugue figure from France, dated to between 26,000 and 24,000 years ago. Engraved twists are visible on the eleven long, plied cords that hang down from a hip band, with the fraying ends at the bottom of each string also clearly depicted.

Among female figurines found in Gravettian Kostenki and Pavlov sites (Russia) are a number which have body decorations that appear to be elements of plaited and woven clothing. Some are belts, some look like bandeaux, others are straps going over the shoulders with finely engraved detail that is reminiscent of open twining.

The well-known Willendorf figure from Moravia, from this same time period, has significant patterning on her head. Although some researchers believe this may represent beads or shells stitched into her hair, it has also been suggested that she's wearing a fibre-based spirally or radially handwoven item, possibly initiated by a knotted centre, similar to coiled basketry. There are similar markings on a number of heads from Kostenki and Avdeevo sites (Russia); the top central part of one from Kostenki looks less like coiling and possibly closer to crossweave or twining.

This early evidence for ancient weaving suggests the technology was not in its infancy; it seems likely that its origins are considerably older – already an established tradition – to appear so fully formed in the Upper Palaeolithic

→ (*Top*) Bone and antler needles made by author using flint and stone tools

→ (*Bottom*) The Lespugue figure, c. 24,000–26,000 years old, France

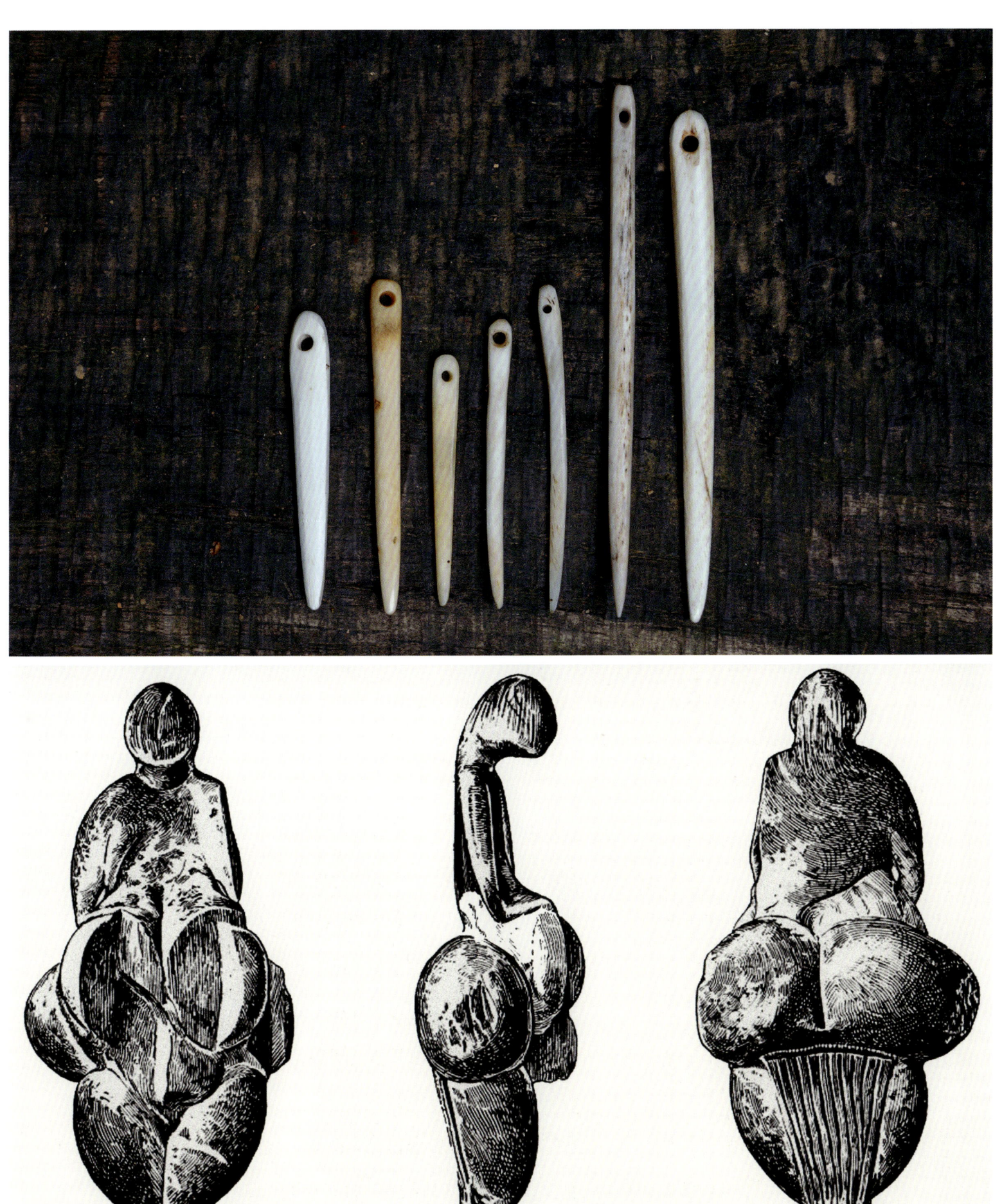

The Brassempouy figure is a small, carved ivory fragment of a head from France, from 25,000 years ago. There is a chequerboard-like pattern on the head, formed by shallow carved lines at right angles to each other. Some interpretations are that it represents hair styled in cornrows, others that she is wearing a flexible open-twined structure fitted over the hair. There's not enough detail on the sculpture to be sure, because it's stylised and indistinct, but it could be split ply or knotted netting.

Less-direct evidence from this period comes from fragments of artefacts with geometric designs incised on them, which are strongly suggestive of weave patterns. A needle case and adzes from Avdeevo in Russia dated to 23,000 years ago; from nearby Kostenki, fragments of bone or ivory bracelets engraved with geometric patterns very much like twill weave; and in Patne (India) a 25,000-year-old fragment of ostrich eggshell incised with a cross-hatch pattern.

During the Gravettian era, the biome was primarily cold, dry grassland. A wide variety of grasses and sedges, herbs and willow shrubs would have been plentiful, all of which yield useful fibres. There is growing evidence that points to boreal (cold-tolerant coniferous tree species) and temperate trees occurring across the region.

All of these finds show obvious skill, which means there was surely considerable prior development. Basketry is unlikely to have emerged fully formed in these contexts, so what evidence exists for precursors to this?

← (*Top*) The Willendorf figure, c. 30,000 years old, Moravia

← (*Bottom*) The Brassempouy figure, c. 25,000 years old, France

A wide variety of grasses and sedges, herbs and willow shrubs would have been plentiful, all of which yield useful fibres

Antecedents

Between 100,000 and 70,000 years ago in Southern Africa, humans were moving into coastal environments. The caves of Blombos and Sibudu in South Africa yield evidence of significant numbers of large fish bones and other marine animals, suggesting intentional catches rather than scavenged food. This in turn suggests sophisticated fishing technologies such as seaworthy rafts, harpoons, nets and containers to carry the catch back to the cave sites. Many of these require other advances like weaving technologies, bone tools and complex composite tools.

At Sibudu there is also extensive evidence of sedge species. Sedge is still used for weaving traditional Zulu sleeping mats. Although there is no direct evidence of mat weaving at Sibudu, there are claims of its likelihood because that time period is believed to be one of increased technological skill. There are fragments of ochre and ostrich shells found at the sites, which are incised with patterning of oblique and horizontal lines, resembling trellis, diamond-like patterns. These are similar to the Patne fragments and other finds at the Upper Palaeolithic Eurasian sites described earlier.

In South Africa at the Diepkloof Rock Shelter, ostrich shell fragments with cross-hatched patterns engraved onto them have been dated to 70,000 to 55,000 years ago. These 270 marked shell fragments are thought to come from at least 25 different water container shells. Traditionally, indigenous people of the Kalahari carry their ostrich egg water containers in netting, and this suggests that the geometric patterns evoke this fibre technology used in their transportation. Many similar incised shell fragments have been found in other parts of South Africa and Namibia from the same period. As Helen Anderson notes in *Basketry and Beyond, Constructing Cultures*, rather than these marks being evidence of symbolic, abstract thought, as is often suggested, they can be understood as a motif with roots in an established visual culture. They relate to patterns already in the visual and cultural repertoire of the maker – weaving, basketry and nets – which are all practices of a subsistence way of life.

Another interesting potential antecedent to consider is in the migration of early humans to Australia. People appear to have arrived on the continent by sea during a period of glaciation around 60,000 years ago, travelling

Traditionally, indigenous people of the Kalahari carry their ostrich egg water containers in netting

→ Netted bags. Left to right: phormium, rush, dandelion, phormium

across water from what's now known as Eastern Indonesia, making them some of the world's earliest mariners. Although we have no specific evidence, they surely would have used fibre technologies to enable that journey, possibly travelling in canoes (crafts with sails of plaited leaves), bringing containers with them – perhaps fibre baskets or bags.

In the next chapter, I look at the link between regional ecology and the emergence of basketry traditions, including a discussion on the universality of techniques through time and place.

→ Coiled baskets. Left to right: crocosmia, grass, iris and honeysuckle, daylily, grass (x2)

↓ Cordage samples made from stems, bast and leaves

ORIGINS: HUMAN ARCHAEOLOGY OF BASKETS AND CORDAGE

FEATURED ARTIST
Chris Drury

Redwood Vortex was commissioned in 2005 by Villa Montalvo in Saratoga, California. The gallery is at the bottom of the track that leads up through the redwood forest above it. This work was part of their outdoor sculpture programme and was included in the exhibition, 'Whorls'.

As I began to be asked to make works outside, I decided to scale up the basket and weave with my entire body, making structures that you could enter, so that there was both an interior and an exterior quality to the work, not something you just contemplated from outside. For these works I invented the weave, a kind of giant fish trap. The work was actually made from willow and poplar, using very thick branches that have a tensile strength.

The vertical sticks cross behind, in front, and so on. There are an uneven number of sticks, so the transverse weave forms a spiral running up the work (an even number of uprights gives you ascending rings of cross weave). Where the uprights cross, you tie them with a transverse weave of two sticks, which weave inside, outside, inside… all under huge tension. There is only one leading edge, so really only one person can make this, although on *Redwood Vortex* three of us worked in unison as the sticks were so thick it needed the strength of all of us together. We wore harnesses clipped onto the scaffolding for safety. As the uprights run out, you push another stick in; the same with the transverse pairs. You make the shape by using rope to pull the structure in.

Redwood Vortex was 22 metres (72 feet) high, made from the top down. The top is delicate, so it was woven on the ground then lifted into position at the top of the scaffolding, which we had erected around the tree. Then the weaving continued from the top to the ground. As you work downwards the gaps get larger, so you begin to weave in thicker sticks, tying onto the scaffold as you go. At the end, we took off the ties and dismantled the scaffold, leaving the work free-standing. There is no rope or string holding it together; just the weave of the willow, and it is incredibly strong. These works are ephemeral and have a life of three years maximum before they become very fragile.

← Body Weaving – *Redwood Vortex*, California, 2005

Chris is an environmental artist making site-specific nature-based sculptures, often referred to as 'land art' or 'art in nature'. He also works in art and science. He creates installations inside and makes works on paper, with maps and with mushrooms, as well as digital and video art.

His work makes connections between different phenomena in the world, specifically between nature and culture, inner and outer, and microcosm and macrocosm. To this end, he collaborates with scientists and technicians from a broad spectrum of disciplines and uses whatever visual means, technologies and materials best suit the situation.

chrisdrury.co.uk

CHAPTER 4
Basketmaking Traditions

← Left to right: English ash, willow, hazel and sweet chestnut

How Traditions Evolve

Making is an innate animal impulse and as humans we're part of that continuum. Across time and place, basketmaking is an indigenous human craft; for millennia we have explored plant materials and techniques to create a myriad of basketry forms in response to need and creative impulse. Almost everywhere in the world, people have used basketry for fundamental purposes in daily life; purposes such as harvesting and processing food, storage, shelter and protection.

It has historically been a subsistence activity: making baskets close to where they were used, from locally harvested materials. These indigenous traditions reflect the ecosystems and flora of a specific region. The maker's relationship to the ecology of their place becomes intimate: in order to make baskets from plant fibres, a detailed knowledge of the landscape and the seasons is needed as well as knowing when to harvest materials and understanding about shrinkage, drying and storage.

Basketmaking techniques developed in response to plant structure and characteristics, with pliability and strength being key. Ideally, the plant material is also long so that there aren't too many joins required in the making, as joins slow the making process and may cause weaknesses in the structure. However, fine, short and weak individual stems can be bound together or plaited to create lengths for coiled baskets. Hard materials like tree branches or trunks (which have both length and strength) can be split until they're thin and pliable enough to weave. Soaking, boiling or dry heating the woody material can shape it and make it more flexible. Specific qualities of materials give rise to certain making techniques which are found worldwide.

Different forms of container emerged as a result of material explorations (marrying techniques and available plant fibres) but also as solutions to particular needs. For example, the carrying of goods, babies, trapping food, sowing seeds, crossing waterways… there's a truly endless

Traditions and cultures are locally formed on the basis of the natural resources, local conditions and practical needs

variety of possible basketry items. Thus traditions and cultures are locally formed on the basis of the natural resources, local conditions and practical needs.

There are also universal traditions. For example, reed boats are known on every continent, and in many separate contexts the ways they are constructed and designed are quite similar. Whether the concept was spread by humans as they travelled, or whether similar optimum solutions were reached independently (being mainly determined by the characteristics of the materials) is unknown. It would be an interesting study to track the historical appearance of basketry types through the world with human migration patterns.

Over millennia, many once-wild plants have come to be cultivated and managed to provide a reliable and steady supply of basketry materials. Localised regional cultivation develops according to climate, geology and topography. There are many variable conditions that influence plant growth: the number of daylight hours, temperatures and rainfall. Soil type determines nutrient content and drainage. Altitude, slope, latitude, climatic zones… all of these have influence too. For example, willow is widely cultivated in temperate regions on lower-lying, wetter ground, and on fertile soils that retain moisture.

→ A variety of baskets made with willow bark, rush, bramble, cedar root and splints, grass, daylily, pine needles, ivy, bindweed, iris, crocosmia, wild rose

BASKETMAKING TRADITIONS

Plant Materials and Techniques Used for Basketmaking Worldwide

Plant Materials

It's impossible to compile a complete list of all species, but the most common plants are listed here:

- **Bamboo**: Native to temperate and tropical zones of every continent, excluding Europe and Antarctica.
- **Bark**: E.g. birch, elm, cedar, willow (also the inner bark: bast fibres).
- **Climbing plants and vines**: As well as other similarly useful local plants.
- **Grasses**: Many species, widespread across the world.
- **Palms**: A large family of trees and shrubs, tropics and subtropics; mainly the leaf used for basketry.
- **Pandanus**: Palm-like trees and shrubs, greatest number of species found in Madagascar and Malaysia.
- **Rattan**: Tropical climbing palm native to mainland Southeast Asia, Philippines and Pacific.
- **Reeds and sedges**: Including *Carex/Cyperaceae* and *Phragmites/Arundo*; found in swamps, marshes and freshwater habitats.
- **Rods/withies and wands**: Pliant shoots from trees and shrubs (e.g. willow, cottonwood, hazel).
- **Roots**: Conifers predominantly.
- **Rushes**: *Schoenoplectus* spp. and *Juncus*.
- **Split wood**: Trees that don't produce pliant rods, split into flexible slats (e.g. oak, ash, sweet chestnut).
- **Straw**: Stems of cereal grains.

Basketmaking Techniques

- **Assembly**: Folding, joining, pegging, nailing and lashing together of separate elements.
- **Coiling**: Bundles of fibre (or flexible rods/strips of plaited fibres) stitched together in a spiral.
- **Frame baskets**: Stake and strand method on a pre-formed rigid hoop/frame.
- **Looping and knotting**: Structures made with a single, active element; network of interlocking loops or knots.
- **Plaiting**: Oblique interlacing of strips making an even, flat material. Three-dimensional forms can also be made.
- **Stake and strand**: Stakes are rigid and passive, strands are flexible weavers. The warp forms the skeleton of the basket.
- **Twining**: Passive warp and active weft elements; fine, pliable materials.

← Netted bags. Left to right: rush (x2), phormium, bramble, willow bast, dandelion

Wild Basketry

Indigenous and Traditional Baskets

As my own cultural heritage is of the British Isles, specifically England, in this chapter I spotlight key phases in the history of English basketry and reference the relationship to place, ecology and economics. There are rich traditions of basketmaking in Scotland, Ireland and Wales, all of which are worthy of further reading (see the Bibliography on page 174 for research by experts and makers).

By indigenous, I'm referring to baskets made of local materials for personal or very local use. They tend to be made using available, suitable plants, and their making often requires particular skills and techniques. Historically in England this includes elm, ash, bramble, rush, iris, hazel, willow, linden, honeysuckle, wild rose and grass. There is a rich heritage among traveller people of making baskets from many of these plants.

Although few basketry remains from the distant past are found (except in waterlogged, frozen or arid landscapes), in England there have been a number of significant Bronze Age discoveries that give us clues about early baskets. In the Dartmoor Whitehorse Hill burial was a coiled basket made from lime (linden) bast; at the Must Farm excavations in Cambridgeshire, large willow fish traps and woven wattle were found. Other interesting evidence of plant use from the same era includes the Dover Boat's yew lashings, and honeysuckle bindings at Seahenge in Norfolk. These finds point tantalisingly to what would have been a rich indigenous basketmaking culture in England. In various parts of Eurasia, where localised conditions have been more conducive to the preservation of organic remains and there has been a longer history of human settlement, there are numerous older, important and fascinating basketry finds made of a wide variety of plant fibres.

By traditional English baskets, I mean those made for larger-scale production and for often quite specific uses, such as various fruit and vegetable baskets which were volume measures, the coal baskets of Cumbria, and fishing baskets used for mass catching. Although these may come from the same regions as indigenous baskets, they are made with cultivated plants and follow standardised techniques. But it's fair to say that there isn't a sharp divide between indigenous and traditional; one morphs into the other, as usage and social circumstances change, with financial imperatives to earn larger sums, particularly in relation to significant changes in recent centuries.

The varied landscapes and ecologies of England provide a rich diversity of plants for basketry, as glimpsed in the earlier description of archaeological finds; of those, many have become cultivated in more recent centuries. Willow grew wild in most parts except where soils were too thin or windswept (north and west edges), and willow beds have long been cultivated in river valleys. Rushes were widely available, especially in the eastern coastal districts. Hazel, oak, linden, ash and other coppiced woods provided weaving rods and splits. Lowland arable fields produced rye and wheat straw for coiling and plaiting.

→ *Sussex trug*, sweet chestnut and white willow. Dominic Parrette

↓ *Cumbrian Oak Spelk basket*, oak and hazel. Lorna Singleton

Land and People: Enclosures

The making of indigenous and traditional baskets is intricately interwoven with land use and consequent access to suitable land and plants. Today we tend to think of wild basketry as synonymous with hedgerow basketry, since hedgerows are one of the few freely accessible places to find suitable plants; to gather other wild plants invariably involves seeking permission from a landowner. This was not always so. In England there is a long and complex history of land practices and legislation impacting every aspect of life, including basketry, and so by necessity this is a brief account of key changes.

The earliest English law concerning access to wild plants dates to 1217: the Charter of the Forest ('forest' meaning all types of common land). The Charter stated that wild plants belong to no one, thus establishing the right to forage and gather. For its time and place it was a radical assertion; a time when in southern England, for example, one-third of the land was designated as Royal Forest, reserved for hunting by the monarch.

The Enclosures, beginning informally around the twelfth century, are a significant part of the country's rural history and remain the defining influence upon the English landscape. Land enclosure is the act of cordoning off an area of land for agricultural use. Prior to this, communal pasture land, 'the commons', and woodlands enabled people to graze livestock, collect wood and turf, as part of their rights as commoners. Basketry materials would have been part of what was collected. Enclosure also privatised areas called 'wastes', which included moors, heathland, downland, fens and marshes. Again, many of these landscapes provide important basketry plants.

Over time, enclosure became increasingly a reason for discontent, and in the seventeenth century when land enclosure became part of the parliamentary process, political dissidents in relation to it such as the 'Diggers' and 'Levellers' began to appear.

By the end of the 1800s, about 30 per cent of England's land had been privatised. Enclosure greatly improved agricultural productivity by bringing more land into agricultural use to feed an increasing population, recognised as the agricultural revolution. It also brought significant changes to the local landscape: where there were once large, communal open fields, land was now hedged and fenced off, and old boundaries disappeared. The rural population gradually lost the connection of commonality with the land and, through the consequence of rural unemployment, were forced off the land permanently to seek work in towns. With this came an inevitable breakdown of traditional community ties and decline of rural craft skills. John Clare, English poet, is well known for his celebrations of the English countryside and sorrow at its significant disruption during this period of Enclosure and the accompanying agricultural revolution.

→ *Essex/East Anglian oyster tendle,* hedgerow elm. Jo Hammond

↓ *Whisket, English/Welsh borders,* hazel. Lewis Goldwater

Industrialisation and Basketry

In earliest times, baskets were made by maker-users and itinerant or semi-itinerant seasonal makers. In rural areas, basketry developed into a cottage industry (a task that could be done indoors at times when the weather was too bad for other activities) and small basketry workshops operated for local trade. As human populations grew and trade became more organised, urbanisation began and money economies became more prevalent.

By the Middle Ages, city basketry workshops were well established and guilds were set up for mutual good and protection among makers. In the seventeenth century, patent systems in England ended the guilds' dominance, laws promoting free trade were established and standardised manufacturing industries emerged. Gradually, the guilds evolved into combinations of trade unions, monopolies, training colleges, trading standards offices and friendly societies – some of which still exist today.

The country-to-city migration described earlier provided the workforce that gave strength to the industries of the city. England and Wales's rural population fell from 65 per cent of the population in 1801 to 23 per cent in 1901. Between 1851 and 1901, England and Wales's rural population declined by 1.4 million, while the total population rose by 14.5 million, and the urban population nearly tripled.

Thus England became an urbanised economy with a large urban proletariat dispossessed from the countryside, a highly concentrated landownership, and farms far larger than any other country in Europe. Enclosure of the commons – more advanced in the UK than anywhere else in Europe – was not the only cause of this situation; free trade and the importing of food and fibre from the so-called New World and the colonies played a part, as did the English practice of primogeniture (bequeathing all your land to your eldest son).

Early on in the Industrial Revolution, before road and rail, river management practices of dredging, cutting straight channels, creating locks and weirs, and clearing vegetation to facilitate transportation impacted availability of important basketry plants such as rush and iris. Still today there can be a conflict of interests between waterways authorities and makers who rely on those plants for their livelihood.

With the Industrial Revolution came a huge increase in the need for transport and a much larger-scale production of baskets, which were required to carry coal, wood or materials. They were needed in industrial-scale numbers for agriculture and fishing and sent out for widespread use geographically. Basketmaking shifted to large city workshops that could keep up with the new high level of demand, and with this came a dramatic increase in the cultivation of willow. Baskets were the cheapest available containers, being resilient and adaptable to a wide range of appropriate forms and specialised designs for particular purposes, such as herring swills, herring crans, potato baskets and Covent Garden sieves.

← (*Top left*) *Sussex Frail or labourer's lunch bag*, English rush. Rachel Frost

← (*Top right*) *Kent watercress basket*, willow. Dominic Parrette

← (*Bottom*) *Devon Stave baskets*, ash, elm, Douglas fir. John Williamson

Twentieth-century English Basketmaking

In England, at the beginning of twentieth century, there were thousands of makers and growers producing baskets for specific functions for both industry and domestic life. Vast numbers of basketry items were made in specialised workshops with locally grown materials on a scale that's hard to appreciate today. This was when the English basketmaking industry reached its maximum size.

In the early part of the twentieth century, European-imported baskets depressed demand for locally produced baskets, but during World War II demand increased again through government contracts for specific baskets. Following the war, production of baskets declined hugely, and modern materials began to replace traditional baskets. After the war, swathes of species-rich coppice that had provided valuable basketry materials were removed across the country and replaced with conifer plantations.

The modern petrochemical industry introduced plastics for bags and containers of all kinds, serving agriculture, fishing, industrial and domestic needs. Cardboard boxes and the now ever-present metal shopping trolleys also took the place of many baskets, and the large-scale cultivation of willow drastically declined. All of this, along with cheaper, imported baskets from Eastern Europe and East Asia, meant that by the 1980s the once ubiquitous basketmakers' workshop was more or less gone across England.

Basketry Heritage in the Twenty-first Century

In the last few decades, there has been an upsurge of interest in and concern for the continuation of traditional crafts, including basketmaking, with the establishment of organisations including the Basketmakers' Association and Heritage Crafts Association. An acute awareness of the possibility of these skills disappearing (it takes only two generations for knowledge to be lost) has been at the forefront of many basketmakers' minds. Like other crafts, basketmaking involves 'tacit' knowledge, which is hard to record through writing or film and can only really be passed on through one-to-one transmission.

In England, a lack of funded training pathways and the devaluation of manual work in society have been contributing factors to the situation. In many schools, creative and practical subjects are excluded, which has reduced young people's craft aspirations.

In 2003, UNESCO adopted a Convention for the Safeguarding of Intangible Cultural Heritage, which includes 'traditional craftsmanship'. It states the importance of 'creating conditions that will encourage artisans to continue to produce crafts of all kinds, and to transmit their skills and knowledge to others'. In 2024, the UK government finally joined this convention.

With issues of supply and provenance, and ecological concerns for a lower carbon footprint, there's a rise of basketmakers cultivating their own materials, particularly willow. As well as many landowners choosing to revitalise coppice woodland, UK government initiatives are supporting its restoration as part of biodiversity and net zero goals, along with a recognition of the associated traditional coppice crafts, including basketry.

As discussed in Chapter 1, there's a widespread, growing appreciation of indigenous and traditional practices in the face of digitalised lifestyles, a recognition of the human need for manual creativity and a sense of belonging to place and to the natural world.

Heritage is what we inherit from the past and what we value and pass forward from generation to generation; it's a living, dynamic thing. Basketmakers around the world have always experimented and adapted to the changing circumstances of social, cultural, ecological and economic contexts. The innate drive to create and innovate will always continue.

Heritage is what we inherit from the past and what we value and pass forward from generation to generation; it's a living, dynamic thing

Wild Basketry

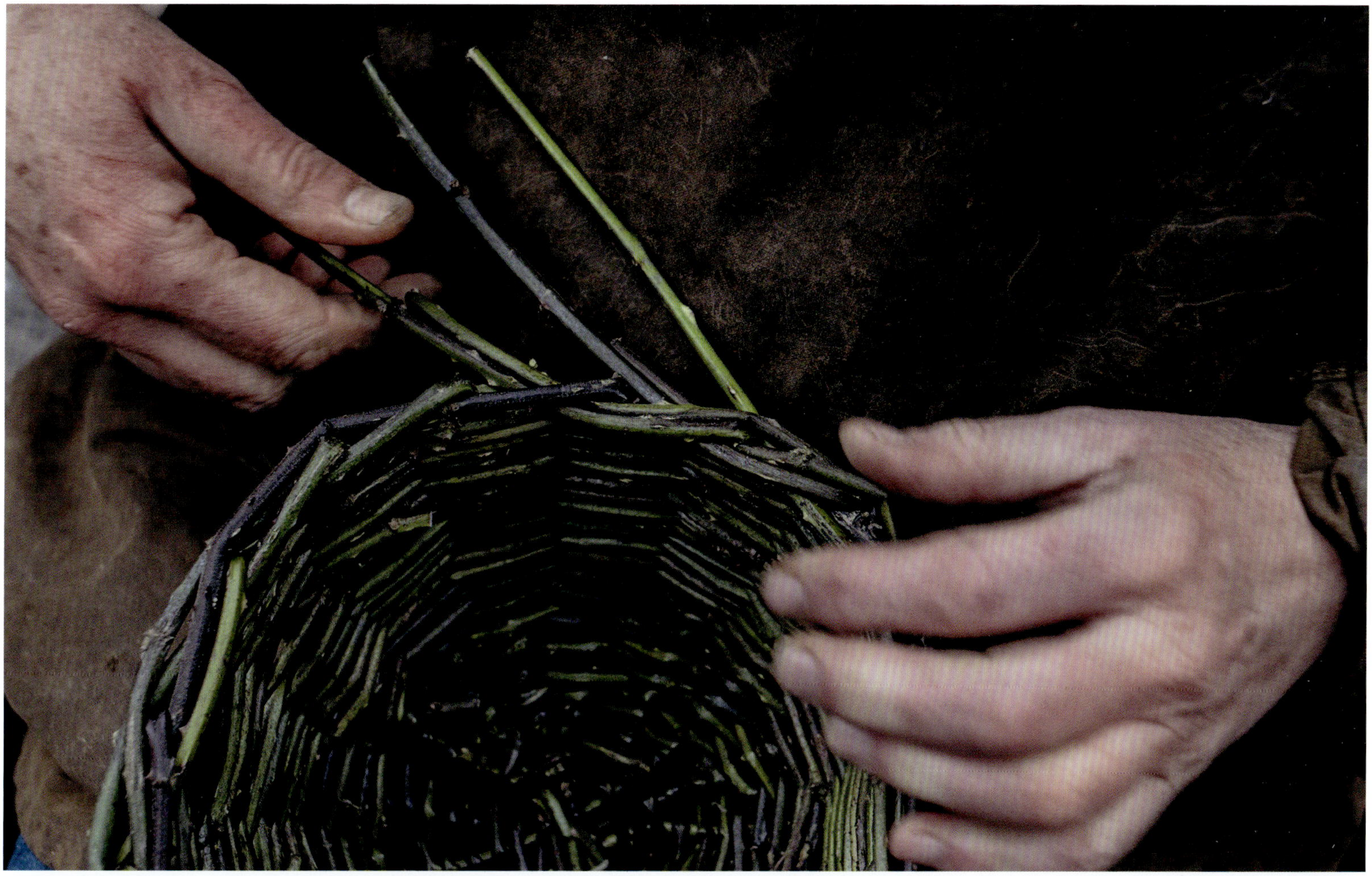

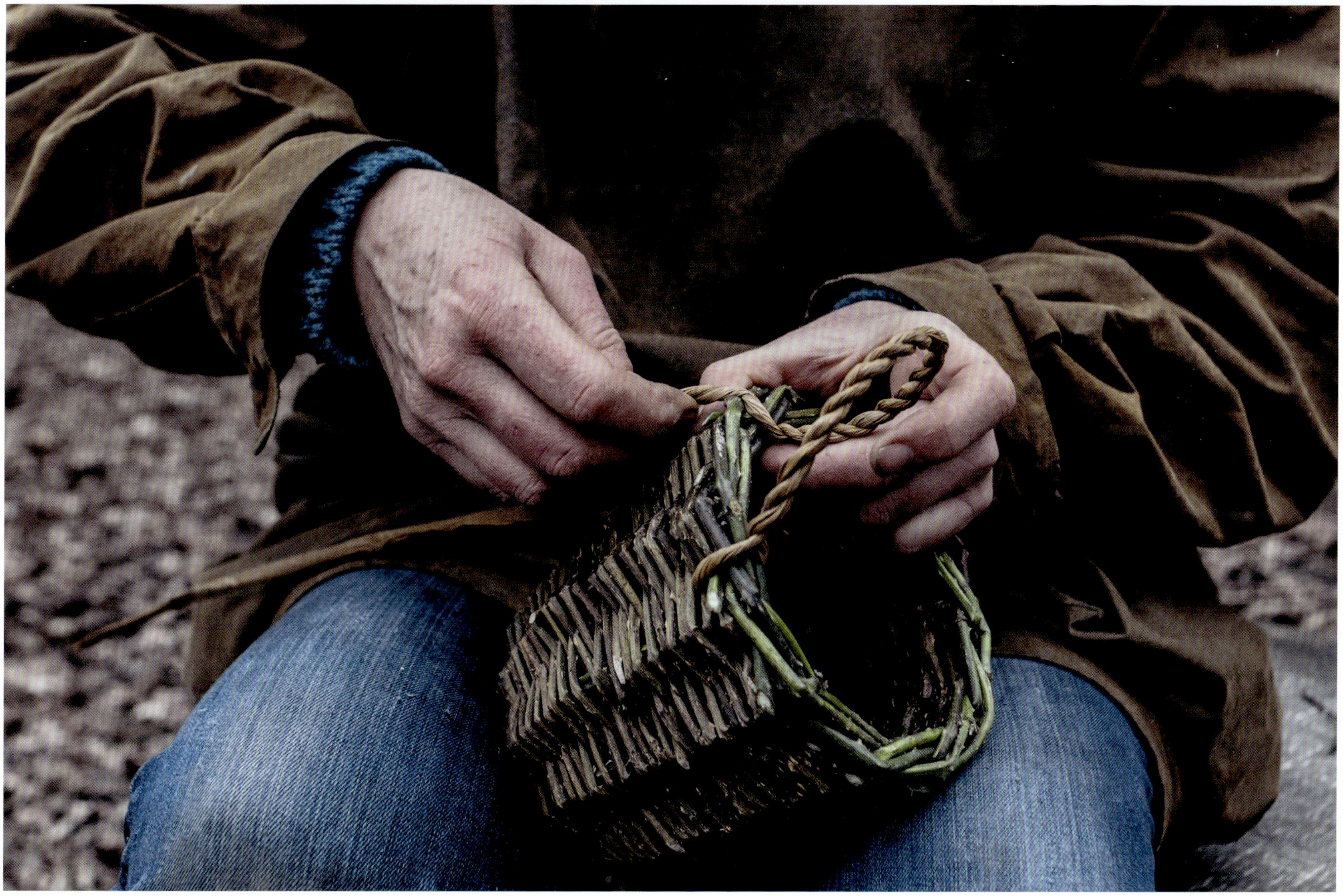

Hazel Holloway, Wakehurst

Walking through Pearcelands Wood at Wakehurst on a quiet, mid-winter day. An open awareness of the trees, plants, creatures; the light and the weather; open to what might present itself as an idea for a new piece.

I'm interested in relationship to place, to the community of plants and animals already there. How to work with minimal impact, to create with my own hands something of beauty that's harmonious, celebratory and in relationship.

Pausing to soak up the sight of majestic oak and beech trees… multiple layers of texture, bare branches, subtle winter colours. A holloway – a sunken path made from centuries of human footfall – on the downwards slope of land, at the bottom a dark yew tree frames a bright circle of green pasture beyond. I envisage hazels either side of the sunken path reaching across to entwine, a series of arches, leading towards the light and space.

Returning in February with a pair of secateurs, small handsaw, flask of hot tea, I explore bending and interweaving the coppiced hazel – much of it seven or eight metres tall – from either side of the holloway. Weaving follows the growth pattern of the hazel to create a relaxed but stable structure. None of the material is contorted, twisted or wrapped tight. Wherever honeysuckle grows through the hazel, I incorporate it.

Occasionally I use extra honeysuckle to secure the hazel, but no other binding or securing – a simplicity of materials that is satisfying and congruent. My focus is on having a light touch with the weave, leaving minimal evidence of human intervention, so that the arches look almost as if they were naturally growing this way. I space the arches with attention to the rhythm of the interlude between each as you move along the path beneath them, to the changes of light and space.

In the quiet of the woods, walking beneath a sequence of seven arches, gradually moving towards an open space in the distance, there is stillness, reverie. Sensing how the light changes between these woven, growing arches; hearing rustles of wood mice in the leaf litter, song thrushes singing from the top of an oak. Maybe we lose ourselves as we enter this suspended space, reconnecting to where we truly belong, within the whole Earth community, or as Antony Gormley puts it, within the 'wider world of creatureliness'.

In April we spot the mossy clump of a nest tucked away high up in one of the hazel arches. A thrush sits incubating her eggs, her tail just visible. And in August we see a wren's nest in another of the arches; there are several chicks in it.

'Make a poem that does not disturb the silence from which it came'
Wendell Berry

→ Overleaf: Hazel Holloway, Wakehurst, 2023
(*Top left*) February, (*Bottom left*) April,
(*Top right*) June, (*Bottom right*) December

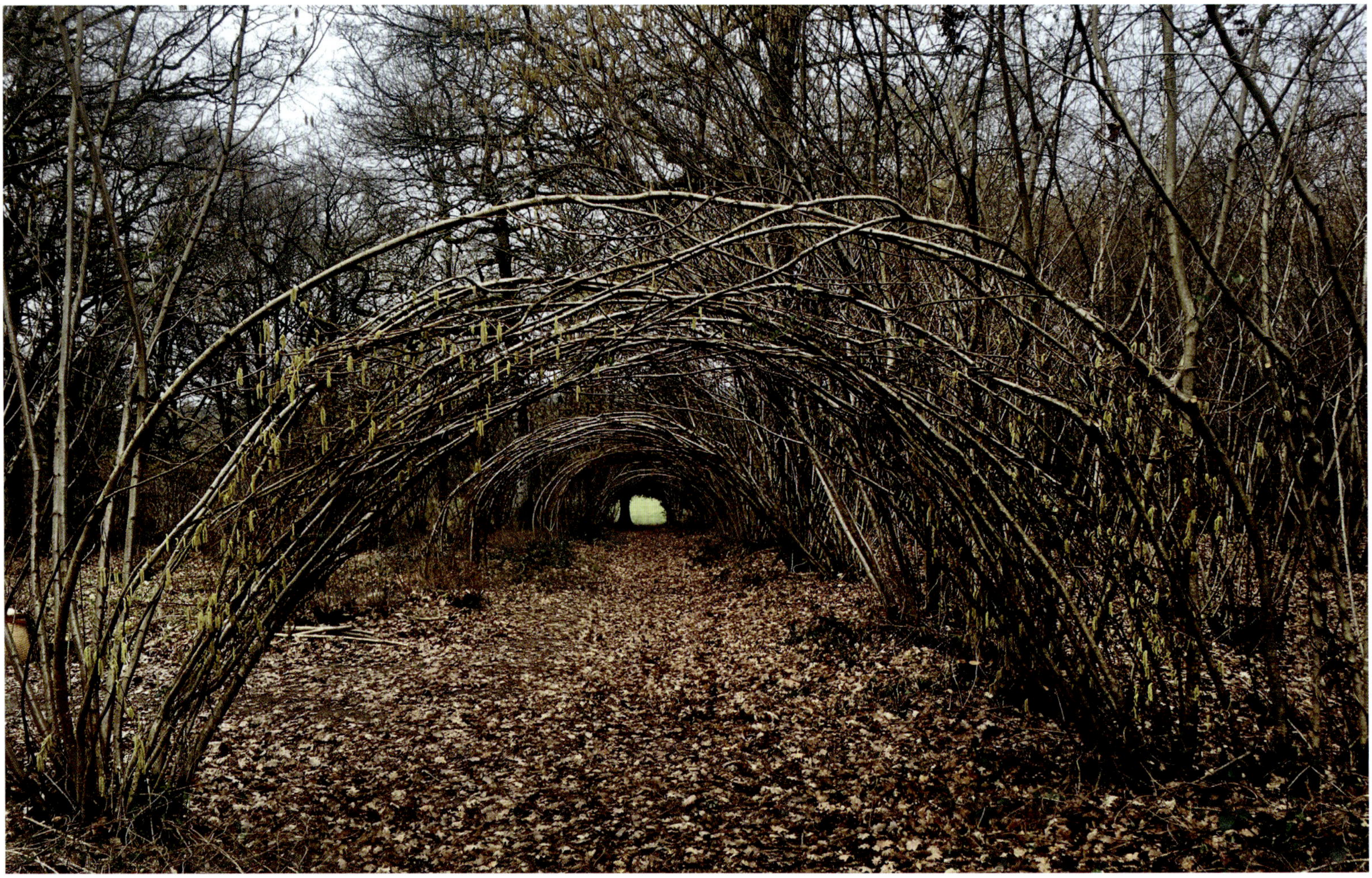

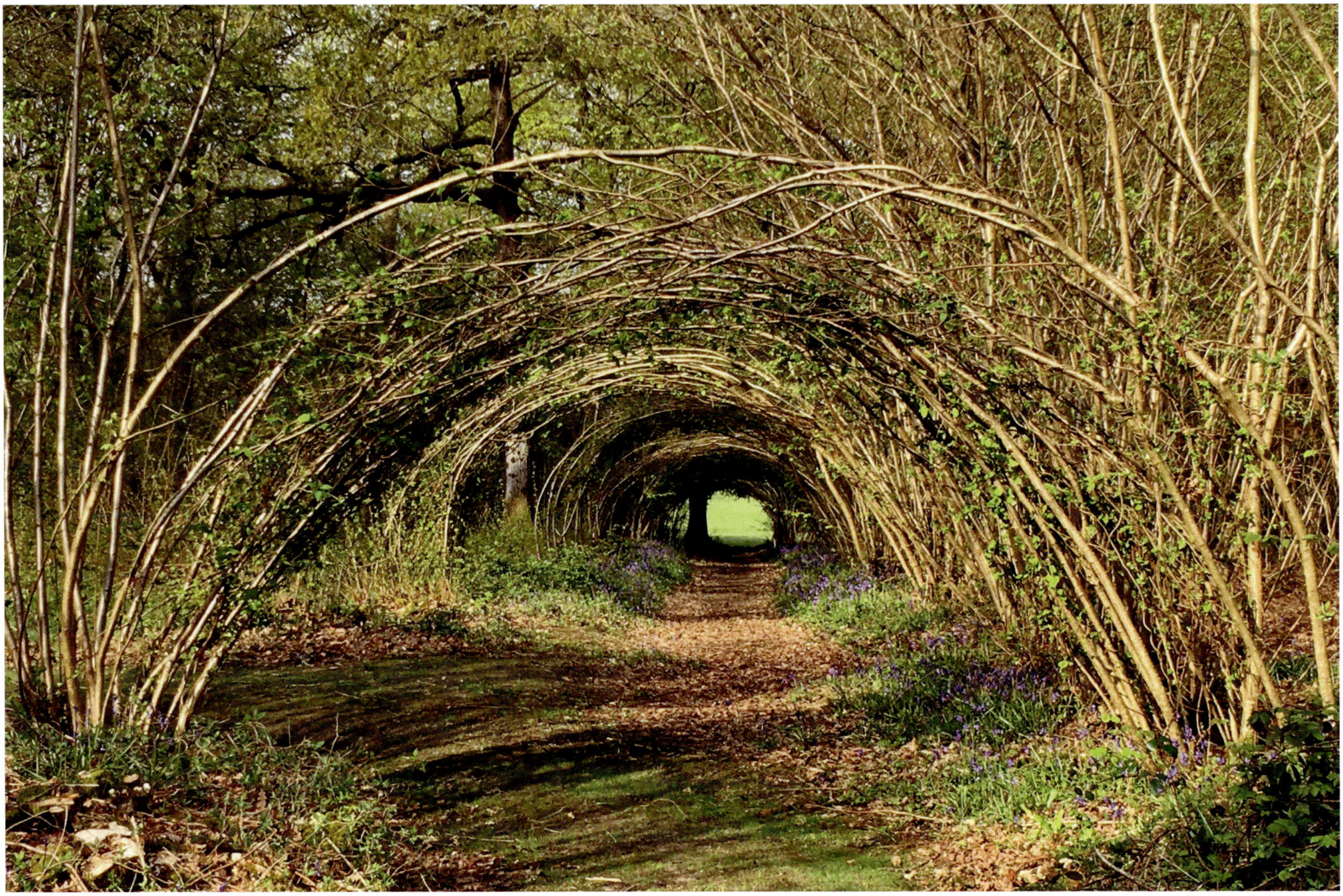

CHAPTER 5

Harvesting Materials

← Harvesting reed mace in summer

There's an arable field margin under two ancient oaks that is species-rich with tall grasses because it has never been cultivated. I've been keeping an eye on the grasses' growth over the summer and I time my harvest to the weather patterns and the setting of the seed. But first I stand and greet the place, the plants and creatures, and offer thanks to the soil, rain, winds and sun, and to the human teachers I've learnt from. A buzzard calls overhead. I scatter some oat grains as a gesture of thankfulness.

The armful of grass I cut gives off a sweet scent, reminiscent of days playing in hayfields. Out on the windswept pastures there's a wire fence where cleavers grow, perfectly dried for fire-making tinder. Their burrs stick fast as I rhythmically pull and bundle the plants. Back in the studio I find I'm covered in the small sticky balls; they're in my socks, even inside my sleeves. As I pick them off and toss them under the nearby hedge, I envisage their spring growth next year that I'll harvest for a medicinal tonic.

In the damp woods I check whether the sap has risen enough for the willow bark to release with ease. My knowledge of the stands of willow there has become more intimate: how one stand in the hollow takes up sap later than the stand on the southerly bank. The repetitive call of great tits echoes through the trees as I work and I notice deer tracks on the small muddy path. Removing bark from the willow rod I've cut, there's a gentle 'pop' as it comes away and I lick the bare wood to taste the sap. My fingers and nails are stained by the tannins in the bark, and by the end of the morning my hands and forearms have the familiar ache from repetitive working.

It takes time to get to know which plants will yield useful fibres in a place. It's a relationship that evolves, requiring an understanding of many different elements. Observing which plants grow where; recognising the various soil and weather conditions that influence this; how the seasons are in a particular year, or were the year before; habits of other creatures who depend on the same plants. You observe signs of those animals, of what else grows nearby, becoming familiar with the communities of plants there. All your senses are fully engaged in this evolving relationship.

→ Reed mace

You develop a mind map of the place, and a sensory map. On regular routes of travel and wanderings in the area where I live, this map has continued evolving: seeing in more detail what grows where, how the wild rose in the hedge that's been cut by the farmer grows better on the other side; how the berry-rich hedgerow on the south-facing clay-rich field, full of insect life, yields particularly vigorous rose whips. I choose and cut them carefully to encourage new growth for next year, and to allow plentiful fruiting. The sharp thorns catch on my clothes and skin.

This year was good for vegetative growth because of the wet, mild spring we had, so the reed mace is healthy and abundant in the ditch. I cut an armful, leaving plenty behind, including the ones that have signs of wainscot moth on them; it's late in the cutting season but some may not have pupated yet. Separating out the reed mace leaves to dry, their clear, mucilaginous gloop covers my fingers and leaves shimmering trails on my clothes.

Somewhat like the basketmaking itself, foraging is an activity that has its own rhythm: it can't be rushed, and the time it may take is unpredictable. It's a case of tuning in and responding accordingly. The eyes take time to acclimatise, the need for something sharpens the seeing. So, at first, all you see is a wild mass of brambles growing on the woodland floor, snagging your ankles. But then you notice last year's mossy blackbird nest hidden deep among them, and the more you look, brambles that are useful for weaving become discernible. Then you notice some small early-flowering wood sorrel, and at the foot of the mossy oak grows a carpet of delicate moschatel flowers, an ancient woodland indicator species. Unseen wood mice rustle and squeak in the abundant leaf litter.

Meandering through the coppice looking for hazel rods, you begin to perceive which are truly straight and the right diameter for setting into basket hoops. A ripe, rotting smell from the leaf litter rises, the winter song of a robin is in the air, blackbird alarm calls announce your presence. All this gives a sense of place among other life forms, you feel a belonging; it is balm to the species' loneliness in a human-dominated world. As Robin Wall Kimmerer says, 'when you know the plants, you just feel more at home wherever you go'.

Keeping integrity and responsiveness in this relationship, there are often times when I can't harvest what I went out for. Perhaps the plants I had in my mind map haven't flourished this season so I don't gather them. Sometimes landowners change how they manage an area, cutting back or clearing, and there is nothing for me. Maybe something else will show itself or possibly nothing will that day. It requires me to be centred, quiet and awake to the place, the plants and animals, the weather and other elements. I must put aside my own time frame, and my attachment to outcome.

→ Wild grass

Humans as a Keystone Species

Biologists and ecologists describe species that have a disproportionate influence on the ecology of their surroundings as keystone species. These are species that shape and modify landscapes by intervening in various ways with the life cycles of plants and other animals, and in doing so increase biodiversity. The wolves of Yellowstone National Park, USA, are a well-known and fascinating example of this.

When plant-gathering, humans behave as a keystone species; we are engaging in ways that enhance the plants we gather and the places where we gather them. When our actions are most beneficial for the overall ecology of our surroundings, as well as for ourselves, biodiversity and people can flourish.

Where I live in Sussex, in the south-east of England, coppiced hazel woodlands are common. It's an ancient woodland management practice that yields long, straight stems of hazel for all types of weaving, including baskets and hurdles, and it dates to at least Neolithic times. When an area of hazel is coppiced, glades are opened up, and in the new light, brambles and many other woodland plants can grow. This brings insect life, which in turn attracts birds and other animals. The basketmaker harvests brambles and hazel rods, which keeps areas clear for other plant species. Blackberries and hazelnuts in such a coppice are offered to us as a way to disperse the plants; our eating of them means that both species – humans and plants – prosper. When we leave enough for the other animals who rely on them as a food source, they too thrive and biodiversity is supported.

Wild Basketry

Good Practice for Harvesting

For wild basketmaking, we're harvesting native or naturalised species that are already growing alongside all the other plants and animals living there, which is different from cultivating or farming plants for basketry. We're looking to cut the plants in ways that support their future growth and benefit all the species that rely on them, including humans.

Essential Guidelines

- Don't take the first as it may be the last.
- Look to see if the plant is healthy and plentiful.
- Take a small amount here and there.
- Give back through caretaking and/or making an offering.

When I'm cutting brambles for weaving baskets, I need one-year-old stems. I go to a place in the winter woods where I know brambles grow abundantly, and walk around for a while to check on the state of the plants to see how well they've grown, and make my greetings and offerings. The stems I'm seeking are the same stems that will bear flowers and blackberries next year, on which many creatures rely. When the tips of those stems grow long enough to reach the ground, they root to create another bramble plant. I want to make sure there are plentiful weavers and fruits for next year, so as I roam across the widespread patch I'm mindful of how much I cut and from where. Even with such a vigorous plant as this, I'm considering future growth.

Not all plants are the same in their growth patterns; each has its own way of regenerating. With careful observation over time, you find out how important it is to balance what you harvest with what you leave, never taking more than half. The laws of right harvesting come from experience and past mistakes.

When you're assessing the well-being of the plant population, your analytical mind reads the signs of health and numbers. But the intuitive mind has another kind of knowing that's equally important; it senses generosity – 'take me' – or a reluctance to give.

In *Braiding Sweetgrass*, Robin Wall Kimmerer describes this in the tradition of the Potawatomi basketmakers (Native American people of the Great Plains, the upper Mississippi River and the western Great Lakes region) who weave with black ash wood. In harvesting a tree for basketmaking, the harvester recognises the individuality of each tree as a 'nonhuman forest person' and requests permission by explaining their purpose. The answer may be a no, an unwillingness in the tree that comes from a cue in the surroundings: perhaps there's a bird nest in the branches, or the bark is resistant to the harvester's knife. There might simply be an instinctual knowing that makes the harvester move on without cutting. But if consent is given, a prayer is made and a reciprocating gift is left – in this case, tobacco.

This tradition of harvesting black ash for baskets created gaps in the tree cover where light reached the seedlings, which allowed young trees to grow to the canopy and reach maturity. In places where the basketmakers disappeared or were few, the forest didn't get opened up enough for black ash to flourish. It's possible, then, to take too little. By doing so – by allowing such traditions to die – relationships can fade and the land suffers. Black ash and Potawatomi basketmakers are partners in a symbiosis between harvester and harvested. Ash relies on people as the people rely on ash. This kind of guardianship of another species is an honour, and it is within the reach of each of us in our own locality.

Much of what we use is the result of another's life, a simple reality that's rarely acknowledged in our society. In the baskets we weave, what would it be like to be sensitive to the lives given? When you follow back the thread of a basket through the lives that made it possible, a natural gratitude arises and a wish to pay respect. There are many ways of expressing reciprocity: land stewardship, ceremony, science, art and basketmaking itself. Even paying attention is an act of reciprocity, receiving the gifts with open eyes and an open heart.

Honourable Harvest

By Robin Wall Kimmerer, *Braiding Sweetgrass*

Know the ways of the ones who take care of you, so that you may take care of them.
Introduce yourself. Be accountable as the one who comes asking for life.
Ask permission before taking. Abide by the answer.
Never take the first. Never take the last.
Take only what you need.
Take only that which is given.
Never take more than half. Leave some for others.
Harvest in a way that minimises harm.
Use it respectfully. Never waste what you have taken.
Share.
Give thanks for what you have been given.
Give a gift, in reciprocity for what you have taken.
Sustain the ones who sustain you and the earth will last forever.

FEATURED ARTIST

Martin Hill & Philippa Jones: *Kanuka Circle*

Making ephemeral art in nature that returns to nature, we work only with what nature provides and respond to opportunities as they arise. This parallels the processes that occur in nature. The biggest challenge is to communicate ideas by using visual metaphors. Art is our language, and we feel compelled to express our belief that humans are at a watershed where we must now redesign our operating principles to align with natural systems or head on down the destructive path we are on.

Philippa and I met at a wilderness rock-climbing area thirty years ago and have been collaborators ever since. She was for many years a craft basketmaker and knows how to use natural materials in creative ways. Although we are different in many ways, we work together intuitively. We also have complementary skills. Philippa recognises ideas immediately and has very good practical skills.

Often, climbing trips take us to remote or interesting places, and sculpture-making just naturally follows. Or we may make a journey to specifically create something. Sometimes I am alone, sometimes with Philippa.

We live on a mountainside covered by native Kanuka trees, close to Lake Wānaka in New Zealand's South Island. Our intimate experience of the lake's ecology and with Kanuka trees in particular was the inspiration behind the idea of this sculpture. The mountains of Mount Aspiring National Park are our climbing and art-making territory.

To achieve the *Kanuka Circle* sculpture, many elements had to come together, as in all our work. The shallowness of the lake with sand bars forms an extremely calm lagoon and we foraged dead Kanuka branches, flooded

← *Kanuka Circle*, Lake Wanaka, New Zealand

by the lake. We discovered that glacial clay in the lakebed was ideal to embed the ends of the flexible branches in, when bent into semicircles.

The realisation of this work was pure joy. It was photographed just after sunrise using a low camera and wide-angle lens to capture the reflection of the sculpture and dramatic landscape. The camera was mounted upside down below the tripod, just above water level, for maximum mirroring and to position the circle in the frame, straddling the horizon.

The creative resolution is the result of exploring the properties of the materials and experimenting with them. Through the combination of the prevailing conditions in the environment and the materials found there, the idea itself is within the interconnection of these elements.

Ideas spring from our direct experience with nature as it connects in our minds with research, memory and philosophy. Our focus is on the relationship between human and natural systems, and although the choice of recurring motifs in our practice changes and develops, the methodology is the same as when we began.

Martin Hill was born in London in 1946. He received a Diploma of Art and Design and went on to win a number of design awards while working in London, Nairobi, Sydney and Auckland.

Philippa Jones was born in Auckland, New Zealand in 1950. She studied art history and has been a craft weaver and freelance writer.

Martin and Philippa have been creative partners since 1994. Together, they create ephemeral sculptures in nature, which Martin photographs. They have exhibited in Asia, Europe and Oceania. Their work has featured in books – including *Fine Line: Twelve Environmental Sculptures Encircle the Earth* about their twenty-five-year global project – and films, most recently in the BBC documentary *Nature and Us: A History through Art*, presented by art historian, James Fox.
martin-hill.com

CHAPTER 6

Projects

The original tradition of basketmaking is one that makes use of commonly growing, plentiful plants in the immediate locality. The plants covered in this section are just that, including a couple that are cultivated widely as ornamentals.

You'll find six basketry projects here that introduce the principles of partnering plant types with basketry techniques. The techniques covered are: twining, assembly, coiling, cordage and looping. By experiencing and understanding these principles, you can build on your knowledge as you explore the particularities of the plants that grow where you live.

←Weaving a bramble basket

Timings for Harvesting and Making

You might think that making a basket is just the weaving itself, but at least 50 per cent of the work – sometimes more – comes long before you weave, particularly when you're harvesting wild plant materials. Most plants have a relatively short harvest season, and once cut are dried so that they can be stored and then used at a later date. In some of the following projects the plants are used fresh; in others the plants are cut and then dried. See below for the harvesting and making sequence, and in each project you will find details about cutting and preparing each plant.

Seasonal Sequence of Plants

- **Bramble** (*Rubus fruticosus*): For baskets, cut September–April. Dry, then weave anytime. For cordage, cut June and use fresh.
- **Daffodil stems** (*Narcissus* spp.): Cut May. Dry, then use anytime.
- **Grass** (*Poaceae* spp.): Cut August. Dry, then use anytime.
- **Phormium spp.**: Cut anytime. Process when fresh, then use anytime.
- **Reed mace** (*Typha latifolia*): Cut August. Dry, then use anytime.
- **Willow bark** (*Salix* spp.): Cut June and use fresh.

Projects Sequence

1. **Bramble Basket** (stake and strand)
2. **Willow Bark Container** (assembly)
3. **Cordage** (Phormium, Daffodil, Bramble, Willow)
4. **Phormium Net Bag** (looping)
5. **Lidded Grass Basket** (coiling)
6. **Reed Mace Basket** (twining)

PROJECT 1
Bramble
(blackberry)
Rubus fruticosus

Native to temperate Europe but naturalised in North America and Australasia, the bramble is a common deciduous shrub with trailing, tangled, thorny stems bearing five-petalled, rose-like white or pale pink flowers (June–September). The leaves are prickly and toothed, changing from green to reddish-purple in autumn. The bramble's fruit – the blackberry – develops between July and October and turns from green to red to deep purple-black.

Bramble grows in size up to three square metres (32 square feet). Its hardiness allows it to grow in a wide variety of habitats: woodland, hedges, scrub, wastelands and dunes. The plant easily hybridises and in the British Isles there are more than 300 subspecies. In optimal conditions it will grow 8cm (3.1in) a day in the growing season. When the tip of a long and fast-growing stem touches the ground it takes root, allowing the plant to spread rapidly.

↓ Silver-washed fritillary butterfly foraging on bramble

The Bramble Community

Although many humans consider brambles a nuisance weed, they are a vital part of the ecosystem for many creatures. Throughout the year, brambles are essential to a huge array of wildlife; in fact, to virtually every hedgerow inhabitant. Being semi-evergreen, they offer an important year-round refuge: rabbits conceal their burrow entrances in banks beneath the tangle of brambles, and foxes make their dens among it. With farmed cereal crops now bearing short stems – too short for harvest mice to nest among – brambles growing in tall grass offer an alternative for their woven, cricket-ball-size grassy nests. Other small mammals like voles and wood mice can shelter in bramble from the sharp eye of a kestrel. Nocturnal mammals like dormice can find shelter from tawny owls, woodland night hunters. Weasels and stoats can slip through the bramble tangle in search of rodent prey. Hedgehogs forage for food beneath the thicket. At the sunny edges of bramble, adders bask, able to slide into its shadows if needs be. It's also a habitat for grass snakes, if water is nearby. Frogs, newts and toads seek the cool shade under bramble, finding food or hibernating there.

Blackberry flowers at the sunny edges of the bush are a source of nectar for bees, brimstone, speckled wood and white admiral butterflies, moths and many other insects. Silver-washed fritillary is a famous bramble feeder; green hairstreak and holly blue will also feed on bramble.

Often nettles grow near brambles, and butterfly species that rely on nettles for egg laying and larval food (such as red admiral, small tortoiseshell, comma and painted lady butterflies) also visit bramble flowers as a food source. Several types of moth rely on bramble leaves for their caterpillars' food source, including peach blossom, garden tiger and emperor moths. If you look closely at the leaves, they're often nibbled or stained or have the signs of a leaf miner's tunnels across them. Blackberries are also eaten by foxes, badgers, bank voles, song thrushes and yellowhammers; dormice eat the flowers and fruit.

Bats feed over woodland and open grassland on insects that are active at dusk and at night. The wren, whitethroat, blackbird and blackcap are among the many birds that build nests in bramble, with plenty of insects around for the insectivorous birds. Dunnocks, song thrushes, long-tailed tits and many warblers also build nests in the dense heart of the bush, knowing that most foxes, cats and crows won't reach them.

The acorn that falls among bramble has a far better likelihood of growing to a tree as it benefits from the same thorny fortress that the birds chose to utilise, as do other tree saplings.

In human health, herbalists value the astringency of the leaves for strengthening the gums, treating mouth ulcers and cystitis, and easing diarrhoea. Blackberries are a popular berry to forage from the hedgerows in late summer, staining tongues and fingers purple. They can be eaten and prepared in numerous ways: eaten straight off the bramble bush or made into fruit leather, desserts and jam.

In natural dyeing, the leaves and fruiting canes of brambles give fawn, grey and yellow-green hues. Blackberries make a lilac colour.

Bramble is often woven into frame baskets, but most traditional stake and strand techniques used for willow can be applied to brambles – at least on a small scale. Brambles are split to make binding material for coiled bee skeps, and these split strips can also be woven into baskets. Its strong fibres are really useful for cordage-making.

↓ Bank vole eating blackberries

Bramble Basket

This basket uses the stake and strand technique

You will need:

- Twenty-four bramble stems 1m (39in) long, diameter 5mm (0.2in)
- Secateurs
- Heavy-duty gloves
- String
- Bucket
- Brick
- Hessian or old towel
- Small craft knife
- Tape measure

Harvesting

Harvest bramble between September and April.

1. Cut long, straight bramble stems about 5mm (0.2in) in diameter, without side shoots, which are one year's growth. Choose stems that don't taper too much and are at least 1m (39in) long.

2. Wearing heavy-duty gloves, run your hand up and down the bramble stems to remove thorns and leaves.

3. Roll the brambles into a loose ring, tie with string, and hang somewhere dry and airy for 2 weeks.

Making

4. The evening before, submerge your dried brambles in a bucket of warm water, weighted down with a brick. Leave for 4 hours. Take out and wrap in hessian or old towel. Leave for 4–6 hours in a cool place.

Weaving the Base

5. Cut eight pieces of bramble measuring 55cm (21.6in) each. They should all be of a similar thickness, about 5mm (0.2in) in diameter. These are your stakes.

6. Find the midpoint of one stake using a tape measure. With the tip of your knife, pierce a hole at that point, gently turning the blade to open up the hole. Slide this pierced stake onto another stake.

7. Pierce a hole in the midpoint of three more stakes and slide them onto the same stake.

Wild Basketry | 93

8. Feed the remaining three stakes up through the four pierced ones, gently expanding the hole as you go. Now you have a cross of four-by-four stakes; this is called the slath.

9. Take two long, thin brambles and trim them to the same length. Poke the tips (thinner ends) into the same hole so that they lie parallel to your stakes and are secure. These are your two weavers.

10. Arrange the weavers as shown – one goes behind the stakes – so that they lie either side of one arm of stakes.

11. The left-hand weaver moves across in front of four stakes, moving to the right (clockwise)...

94 | **Wild Basketry**

12. ... Then it goes behind the next four stakes...

13. ... Then it comes back to the front. Take the other weaver in your fingers.

14. This other weaver now moves in the same sequence: in front of four stakes, behind four stakes and back to the front. You have now completed one stroke of the weave. This weave – called 'pairing' – is used for the whole basket. Take the other weaver in your fingers.

15. Continue the sequence one more time until you're back to where you started and have completed a round. You have now completed the tying in of the slath.

16. Gently separate the stakes and bring the right-hand weaver to the front, between two stakes.

17. Continue weaving. Always move the left weaver first: across in front of two stakes, gently pull it down at the back so that it sits in close, then behind two stakes and back to the front. Turn the work anticlockwise as you weave. When you get all the way around, gently separate the stakes and bring the right-hand weaver to the front between single stakes.

18. Continue weaving, going in front and behind single stakes (always pulling down gently at the back) so that the stakes become like spokes of a wheel.

19. When the weave measures 7cm (2.75in) across, you have made your base.

Adding Weavers

20. When your weavers run out, choose two more that are the same length and thickness as each other. Insert the first new weaver as shown, so 2cm (0.8in) sticks out at the back.

21. Weave the first new weaver in front and behind a stake, then add in the second, as shown. Old weavers will stick out 2cm (0.8in) at the front, and new ones out 2cm (0.8in) at the back. You'll trim them later.

Tip
To keep your weaving as even as possible, the tip of your new weaver should match the thickness of your old weaver.

Shaping

22. To make the sides of your basket, bend the stakes away from you as you weave. Do this gently but firmly so that the stakes gradually change angle. Avoid creating right angles; you want the change to happen over about three rounds of weaving.
23. On your lap, with the stakes pointing away from you, continue weaving up the sides of your basket.
24. Stop weaving when your stakes are 14cm (5.5in) long (the length needed to make the border).
25. To finish, thread one weaver under the previous row of weaving to prevent any undoing. Cut your weavers, leaving tails of 3cm (1.1in) each.

Making a Trac Border

26. The simple trac border is made by the stakes, woven in a sequence of: behind one, in front of one, behind one and back to the front. To begin, use your thumbnail to make an elbow bend in a stake 2cm (0.8in) above the top edge of the weave, as shown. Move that stake, bending it gently as you go: behind one stake, in front of the next, behind the next and back to the front.

27. Do exactly the same with the next two stakes, making the elbow bend and following the same sequence.

28. Continue with all the stakes, but now make sure that the elbow bends are aligned with the top of the border that's emerging.

29. When you have three upright stakes remaining, these stakes will follow the same pattern but their final move will be to come out through the first three elbow bends that you made (see Step 30).

30. Starting with stake 'a', continue the same sequence: going behind one stake, in front of the next, behind the next and back to the front. You will need to carefully thread each bramble through the other stakes as you go.

Finishing

31. Carefully snip all the ends that are sticking out, both inside and outside the basket. Make a long diagonal cut with sharp secateurs.

Tip
Make sure that the cut end of the bramble rests against a stake and isn't so short it slips through to the other side, leaving a gap.

Development
Experiment with other long, bendy woody or semi-woody plants like ivy, dogwood and willow. Prepare them in the same way as for bramble.

Wild Basketry | 101

PROJECT 2

Willow Bark
Salix spp.

Willow trees (*Salix* spp.) are widespread, growing on moist soils in cold and temperate regions. Deciduous, they grow on riverbanks, fens and hedgerows, and widely hybridise with each other. Their roots will readily sprout from a stick put in the ground. Known as a pioneer species, they were one of the first trees to establish in Britain after the Ice Age. The broader-leafed willows (grey willow and goat willow) are often referred to as sallows.

The Willow Community

Salix cinerea, known as pussy willow, has grey, furry buds early in the spring that become nectar-rich, pollen-covered catkins – an essential early food source for many pollinators including overwintering honeybees and early emerging ground-nesting solitary bees. And, because the catkins attract so many insects, early insectivorous, migratory birds also depend on them.

↓ Bee foraging on sallow (pussy willow)

Hundreds of species of invertebrates rely on willow as an essential part of their life cycle, including a high number of gall-producing insects. Sallow growing in partial shade is the preferred food source of the purple emperor butterfly. In spring, the adult Camberwell beauty butterfly – a rare migrant to the British Isles (originating in Scandinavia and mainland Europe) – feeds from sallow flowers, and sallow leaves are the preferred food source for its larvae. Goat willow foliage is also eaten by the caterpillars of a number of moths, including the sallow clearwing, dusky clearwing, lunar hornet clearwing, sallow kitten and puss moth. Bats also feed on insects that are active at dusk and at night, over woodland and wetland areas.

Once willows spread, they form thickets that serve as nesting spots, attractive to bird species that like young open woodland, scrubland and wet woodland. This includes goldfinches, willow warblers and lesser redpolls. Willow tits also prefer this kind of regenerating woodland and they remain on or near their territory all year round. Their population has declined to the point that they have been red-listed in the UK since 2022. Habitat deterioration and loss is thought to be the main factor.

Willow is favoured by beavers to build their dams in freshwater rivers or streams, as it grows abundantly there. Willow bark and leaves, along with poplar and alder, are an important winter food source for them. Beavers are a keystone species, meaning they play a critical role in creating ecosystems from which a wealth of wildlife benefits. By creating dams, making ponds and forming canals to swim around their territory, beavers create a habitat that helps lots of other wildlife to thrive, including water beetles, birds, bats, frogs and fish. Their dams can also prevent flooding further down river, keep water

Wild Basketry

flowing during droughts and even filter the water passing through them.

People traditionally pollard willows at head height (out of the reach of grazing animals) to give a regular crop of poles suitable for fencing and firewood. Osiers (*Salix viminalis*) are coppiced (cut to ground level) to give long, slender stems for basketmaking. Other uses for willow wood are cricket bats, coracle boats, wattle panels for buildings, artist's charcoal and biomass fuel. Willow bark also contains salicin and other aspirin-like compounds for medicinal use.

The leafy stems and bark of willow produce pinkish tan, grey and yellow dye colours. Willow also contains high levels of tannin, which is useful in dyeing processes.

Many other tree barks are valued as materials to craft with: birch bark from trees growing in northerly latitudes produces a thick, pliable bark that feels like leather. Throughout Eurasia and North America it's a highly valued material for traditional crafts including manuscripts, canoes, dwellings, cradles and containers.

Pacific Northwest First Nation peoples weave with cedar bark to make hats, textiles, mats, baskets, nets and ropes. Elm and hickory inner bark has traditionally been used for chair seating in Europe and North America.

↓ Eurasian beaver eating willow

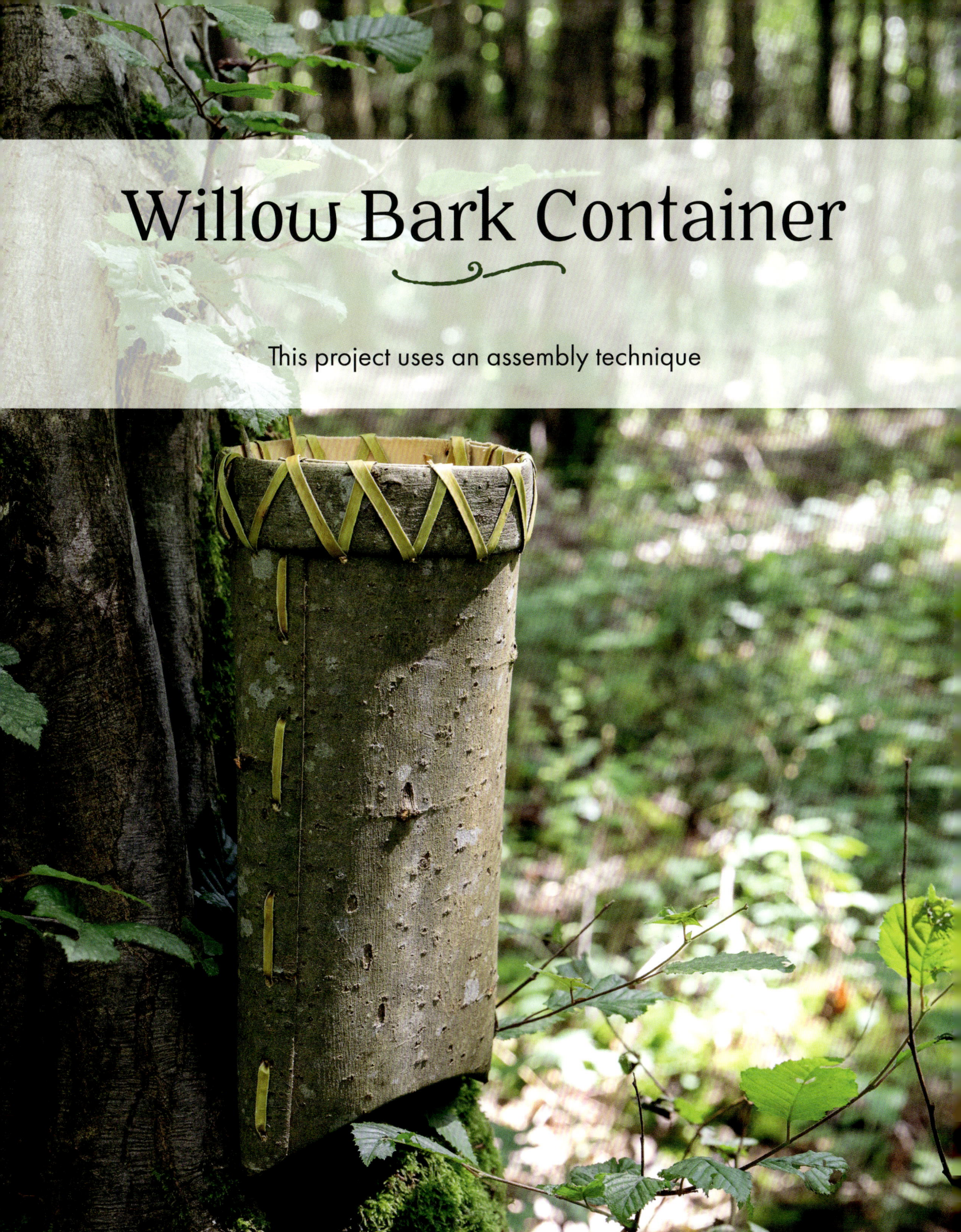

Willow Bark Container

This project uses an assembly technique

You will need:

- Two 8cm-diameter willow branches: 75cm (29.5in) long and 40cm (15.75in) long
- One or two 2–3cm-diameter willow branches, at least 75cm (29.5in) long
- Small handsaw
- Heavy-duty gloves
- Small craft knife
- Ruler
- Pencil
- Strong scissors
- Pegs
- Palm drill

Harvesting

Harvest in mid-spring when the sap has risen and new leaves are well opened. Select a small branch from a pollarded or coppiced tree. Sometimes this type of growth occurs naturally when a tree is felled by a storm. Any willow can be used, but I use goat willow (*Salix caprea*) because it grows abundantly in my area.

1. Choose a long branch of about 8cm (3.1in) diameter that's reasonably straight, free from bark damage and with a healthy amount of leaves at the top. Make sure that you can easily get close to the branch, there's space for it to come down safely when you cut and no people or animals are close by. Saw at the base, with a supporting hand holding the branch, as shown. Most branches will have a slight lean to them; cut on the upper side so that as the branch falls, it falls away from the saw.

PROJECTS

2. Leave a smooth cut edge to protect the health of the tree. Cut your branch down into the lengths you need – reasonably straight and without side shoots. You should be able to cut the thinner lengths you need from the top of your main branch.

3. Measure and cut safely, as shown. Note the angle of the saw blade, which avoids the blade getting stuck. Any branches you don't need should be piled neatly together under or behind the tree to provide habitat and gradually decompose.

Making

4. On your 75cm-long, 8cm-diameter branch, carefully score a straight line down the length with your knife, holding the branch as shown. The base of the branch should be resting on a firm surface (in this case the bench) and not on your leg. Press lightly with your knife so that you stay in control of the blade. Score the line a few times until it goes through the bark to the wood beneath.

Wild Basketry

5. Ease the bark away from the wood all along the cut, sliding your fingers under it and running them up and down the wood to release the bark, until you can get your hands around the wood and the bark comes away.

Tip
Ease the bark away gently and gradually to avoid it splitting. If the bark doesn't come away easily, it's because you've cut your branch either too early or too late in the season and there's not enough sap.

6. With the outer bark facing down, use the ruler to find the midpoint of your material and mark it with a soft pencil line. Mark two points, 3.5cm (1.4in) on either side of this line. Avoid flattening the bark as that will cause it to split. Mark two points on the central line, 2cm (0.8in) in from the edges on both sides. Now draw an ellipse that joins those points and takes in the previous two points you marked. Go over the lines firmly a few times to score the material (taking care not to go through it), then draw two V shapes on the edges, as shown.

7. Carefully cut out the V shapes with scissors.

8. Turn the material over and gently fold the scored ellipse, easing it into shape.

9. With scissors, trim the top ends of your material to be level and cut off any splits. Peg at the top; there will be a 2cm (0.8in) overlap because of the small V shapes you cut out. Your container should be about 28cm (11in) high.

10. Score a line down your 40cm-long, 8cm-diameter branch with your knife as before, then another parallel line to create a strip that is 3.5cm (1.4in) wide. Peel this strip away.

11. Peg this strip securely to your bark container and cut the end to allow a 2cm (0.8in) overlap.

Tip
Put your other hand inside your container to support it and avoid the bark splitting. Take care to keep your inside fingers out of the way of the drill.

12. Mark where you'll drill eight holes up the side of your container. The top hole should be just below the pegged-on rim. Drill the holes using the palm drill, going through the two overlapped layers of bark.

Rim and Stitching

13. Take one of your 2–3cm-diameter branches, score a line with your knife and remove the bark as before.

14. With scissors, cut at least four strips 4mm (0.1in) wide.

Wild Basketry | 111

15. Tie a knot in the ends of two strips. Cut their other ends to a point.

16. Unpeg and remove the bark rim for now. Start at the bottom (with the knot on the inside) and thread the strip through the holes to lace up your container, working on both sides at the same time. Once you get to the top, gently pull out the slack on both strips so the lacing is as tight as possible. Take your time as this is fiddly and slow.

17. Leave the ends of your lacing strips, and re-attach the rim with pegs.

18. Mark out and drill 10 or 12 evenly spaced holes just under the rim all the way round.

19. Secure the rim by threading one of your lacing strips through a hole to the front, going over the rim and back to the outside through the next hole on the right. As you go, gently pull the lacing snug to take out as much slack as possible, and remove the pegs.

Tip
If your lacing material has become dry and stiff, run it briefly through water and leave it wrapped in a tea towel for 10 minutes.

Development
Experiment with other tree barks, such as linden, elm and chestnut. The same harvesting guidelines apply as for willow.

20. When you get all the way round, go back the other way, re-entering the same holes to create a zigzag binding. Your lacing strips may be long enough to complete the binding but if not, add in new strips and finish by knotting them on the inside.

Hanger
21. To make a hanger, use the palm drill to make two holes on the back, as shown. Thread the ends of a thin strip of bark from the inside to the outside of your container and tie a knot on each end.

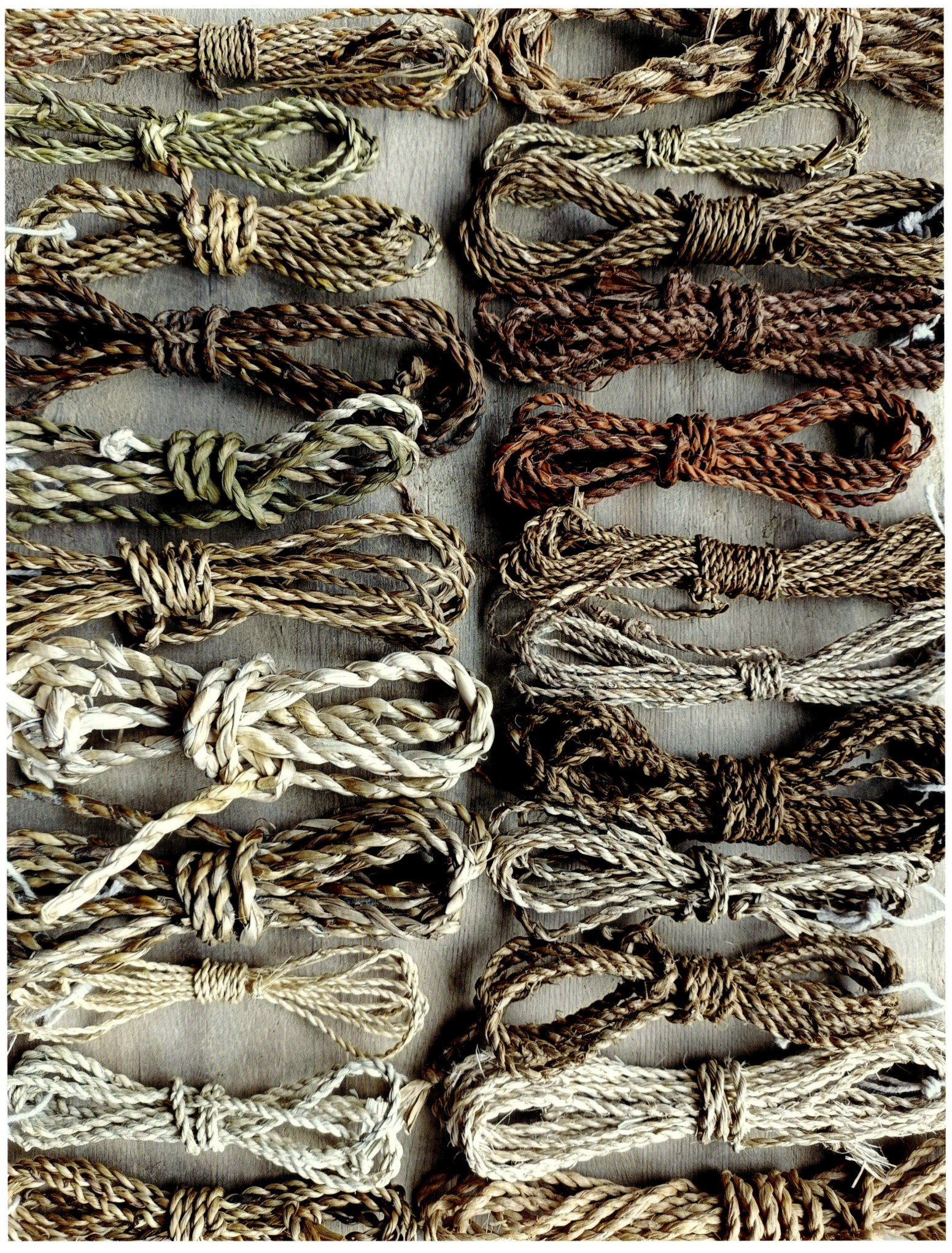

PROJECT 3

Cordage

About Cordage

String, cordage, rope: these are all collections of relatively short, small fibres twisted together into a tight structure that is larger, longer and stronger than any of the original fibres. String is such a fundamental part of everyday life that it's often taken completely for granted. So many items essential to the modern world depend on long stuff that connects one thing to another: cranes, bridges, shoelaces, any kind of woven fabric, electricity cables and lines of all kinds. In fact, such is the importance of cordage that it's considered a human cultural universal.

If you were living before the time when the making of cordage was known, your options for tying anything together would be limited to strips of flexible, strong material of a finite length. In the plant world that could be vines or tough fibres from long leaves or bark. From animals, hide, sinew or gut could provide you with longish pieces of material. All of these would need to be strong in and of themselves and extendable only by tying them together.

But once you know how to make cordage, the twist and counter-twist technology allows you to take individually weaker fibres – lots of them – and make infinite lengths of potentially strong, flexible string and rope (rope is thicker than string). As we saw in Chapter 3, the origins of string-making lie far back in the mists of time. The development of technologies such as the looping and weaving of cordage meant items could be made entirely from string to create a range of objects like bags and nets. These are likely to have revolutionised hunting, fishing and the collection of small items by enabling people to make snares and fishlines, tethers and leashes, carrying nets, handles and packages. Cordage also provides ways of binding objects together to form more complex tools, and creating woven textiles.

Elizabeth Wayland Barber, in *Women's Work*, describes the development of cordage as the string revolution. It would have greatly improved the odds of survival for early humans, paving the way for many significant developments in our material culture.

Wild Basketry | 115

Materials and Making

Plants have historically provided the highest volume of fibres for string- and rope-making. There are so many plants that have twistable fibres: flax, hemp, nettle, ramie, jute, sisal, esparto, agave, yucca, elm, linden, willow, coir, mulberry, honeysuckle, kudzu, milkweed… the list of suitable plants goes on and on. Animal fibres can also be used – hair (human or animal), hide, sinew and gut – and are useful in ecosystems where there are few plant resources.

Depending on the job you want your string to do, and/or what you have to hand, you'll use different fibres. The qualities of a plant's fibres that make the best string and rope are: having good tensile strength (both wet and dry); resistance to abrasion, rot and sunlight; and an ability to withstand heat.

Hemp and flax are prized for having very strong fibres. Historically, hemp has been a primary material for rope-making. It grows 3–4.5m (9.8–14.7ft) in height, thus giving long bast fibres. In large-scale production, the stems are soaked (retted) then beaten to separate the fibres from the core. For netting, flax (linen) was historically preferred, being a softer and finer fibre.

However, Manila hemp (a banana species, abaca, native to the Philippines) and sisal (an agave, a fibrous succulent native to southern Mexico, but widely cultivated and naturalised in many other countries) have become more widespread for rope production. With vast amounts of rope needed for shipping, fishing and other industries, string and rope production is carried out on a massive scale, though always following the same principles as covered in the cordage projects here.

Prior to the Industrial Revolution, rope was most often made by simple twisting. Depending on your need, you could twist a good four metres (13 feet) of two-ply rope in under an hour with no tools other than your two hands. At the other extreme, you could twist ropes strong enough to anchor a ship or bridge a river, several hundred metres (1,000 feet) long, with only a few simple, human-powered tools. It was only in the Industrial Revolution that power came to be used in rope-making.

Since the 1950s, plant fibres have largely been replaced by synthetic fibres. Nylon and polypropylene are twice as strong as hemp or flax, and plastics are also resistant to rotting. However, they pose ecological problems in our world, being a serious threat to aquatic life and birds as well as creating ocean debris and secondary microplastics, another significant risk to health.

Bast

Bast is the inner bark of a woody plant. The bast fibres are just beneath the outer bark (epidermis) within the phloem. To extract the fibres, the wood is generally retted. This means leaving it in water for 6–8 weeks (or longer, depending on temperatures) to allow the necessary microbial action to separate the fibres. Singly, bast filaments can readily snap if you tug at them, but collected as a bundle and given a few twists, they form a strong length of useful string.

The weather elements alone can ret plant material away from the bast fibres. My first bast harvest came from a mature, fallen

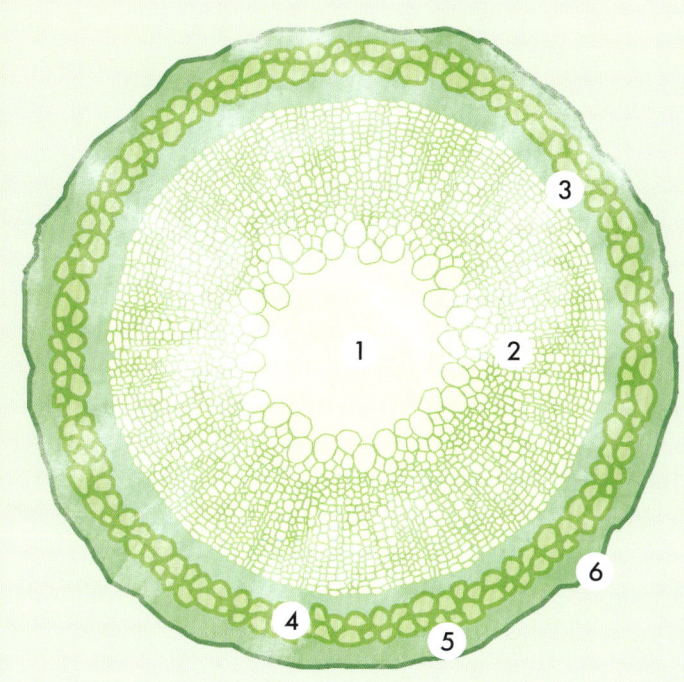

FLAX STEM CROSS-SECTION
Pith (1), xylem (2), phloem (3),
bast fibres (4), cortex (5), epidermis (6)

willow tree whose bark had been weathered in this way. I peeled away the exposed fibres and the amount I gathered made enough cordage to loop a small bag.

Semi-woody plants like nettles and flax can be retted by soaking for a couple of weeks, though they can be easily over-retted this way. Many fibre specialists prefer to ret them by leaving them out in the dew for a few weeks, turning (and checking) daily, so that the useful fibres separate from the plant pulp and woody core this way instead.

Leaves and Stems

Many plants have suitable fibres in their leaves and stems. Depending on the plant in question, methods of stripping, scraping, crushing, beating and brushing are used to get rid of any pulpy material, leaving the sought-after cellulose fibres. Succulents such as sisal and yucca leaves are processed this way for their fibres, and Manila hemp fibres come from the leaf stem of a type of banana plant.

↓ Bramble bast fibres (left) and phormium leaf fibres (right)

Wild Basketry

TWISTS

Twists are internationally described as S and Z based on the direction of the central slant of these letters. If the twist moves away to the left, it is an S-twist and said to be left-handed; if it moves away to the right, it is a Z-twist and said to be right-handed.

How It's Made

Yarn is single ply. Fibres have been twisted together all in the same direction so that the force of the friction grips them.

Cordage (twine, string and rope) is two or more yarns twisted together in one direction and then wrapped around each other in the other direction (a counter-twist). It's the counter-twist that stops any unravelling and creates a consequent strength. Two yarns give you two-ply cordage, three yarns three-ply and so on.

The following projects show you how to make two-ply cordage using the reverse twist, rope lay technique. Other cordage-making techniques include thigh rolling and palm twisting, both of which work best with long lengths of fibre. They're also quick and productive methods once you're confident and well-practised, but I recommend the rope lay technique as your starting point.

By completing all four cordage projects in this section, you'll learn the basic principles of using leaf, stem and bast fibres from different plants so that you can then apply those principles to experiment with other plants. To explore the possibilities of a new fibre for potential cordage-making, three simple tests are applied:

1 Can it stand a little tugging without breaking?
2 Can it be twisted without breaking?
3 Can it be tied in a simple knot without breaking?

If the answer to each question is yes, then the fibre in question is worth experimenting with.

If you're a beginner I recommend you start with the first project (Phormium) because it's a very straightforward process to extract long, even fibres from this plant – perfect when you're starting out.

The quantity of plant material mentioned in each project is enough to make at least a metre of cordage.

Once you're confident with making cordage, the next project in the book shows you how to progress to making a looped cordage bag. Cordage-making is a slow process but with repetition it becomes fluid, automatic and very compelling.

→ Cordage projects left to right: willow, bramble, phormium (x3), daffodil

118 | **Wild Basketry**

Phormium Cordage

Fibres are extracted from phormium leaves

Phormium is an evergreen perennial plant native to New Zealand and Norfolk Island, Australia and its Māori name is 'Wharariki'. The plant grows as a clump of long, sword-shaped leaves up to two metres (80 inches) long. Its dramatic yellow or red flowers grow on tall shoots.

You will need:
- One or two phormium leaves
- Secateurs
- Large sharp needle

Harvesting
Harvest any time of year. There are many varieties of phormium with various leaf colours; any variety/colour is fine for this project.

1. Cut the leaf very close to the base of the plant with secateurs. Cut outer, mature leaves (not the young inner leaves) and trim off the bottom, thicker part. You'll be working with the open leaf part.

Preparation
2. The leaf has a raised rib running down the centre. Halfway along, pierce the leaf with your needle next to the rib and split the leaf by drawing the needle along, first in one direction then the other.

3. Repeat on the other side of the rib. Discard the rib.

4. Use the needle in the same way to split the leaf into very thin strips of fibre, as narrow as you can make them. You can scrape these strips with your thumbnail to remove excess green matter, exposing the paler cellulose fibres.

Making

5. Take a small bundle of split fibres (between three and seven strands). Allow the ends to be staggered; don't line them up. At roughly the midpoint, hold the bundle between your left thumb and index finger. With your right hand, twist the bundle away from you for about 5cm (2in), as shown.

Tip
Make the twist by pulling the pad of your thumb towards you, while holding the fibres between that thumb and index finger. You might need to occasionally dampen your thumb and finger pads to assist with the twist.

6. Bring your hands together and the twisted length will naturally kink to make a small loop, as shown. If it doesn't kink, your twist needs to be a little tighter.

7. Hold the small loop with your left hand so that you have two bundles sticking out to the right. With your right hand, take the top bundle, twist it away from you (clockwise) as before, then bring it down in front of the other bundle, which now becomes the top bundle. Take this new top bundle and repeat the twisting and bringing down. Keep repeating.

8. When you feel one bundle thinning, add in more material: lay in new fibres on the bottom bundle (as shown) then twist the top bundle and bring it down as usual.

Tip
You want your cordage to have a consistent thickness, so add small amounts of fibre frequently.

9. Added-in fibres leave a tail, which you can trim away at the end.

10. To finish, tie a knot in the end. You can make different thicknesses of cordage by having more or fewer fibres in your two bundles.

Daffodil Cordage

The daffodil stem is used for fibres

Narcissus (daffodil) is native to the Mediterranean region, but there are a lot of different species growing in a variety of habitats. Many are considered ancient introductions to central and northern Europe, growing as far east as Iran and Kashmir, and they are also cultivated in large parts of North America.

You will need:
- Around twenty dried daffodil stems
- Bucket of water
- Tea towel
- Small scissors

Harvesting
Harvest in late spring, once flowering has finished. Any type of daffodil is fine.

1. Cut the flower stems at the base of the plant. Don't cut any of the leaves as they'll be feeding the bulb for next year's flowers.

To dry the stems, either lay them out flat or tie the stems in small bundles and hang in a warm, airy place. Drying takes around 3 weeks. Once dry, you can use them whenever you're ready.

PROJECTS

Preparation

2. A couple of hours before use, dunk your dried daffodil stems briefly in a bucket of water.

3. Wrap the dampened stems in a tea towel and set aside for a couple of hours.

Tip
Your material should be just damp enough to manipulate. If your stems are too damp when you're using them, the cordage will dry with gaps in it.

Making

4. From your wrapped bundle, select three stems of different lengths and snip off any flower head remains.

Wild Basketry | 127

5. At roughly the midpoint, hold the bundle of stems between your left thumb and index finger. With your right hand, twist the bundle away from you for about 5cm (2in).

6. Bring your hands together and the twisted length will naturally kink to make a small loop, as shown. If it doesn't kink, your twist needs to be a little tighter.

7. Hold the small loop with your left hand so that you have two bundles sticking out to the right. With your right hand, take the top bundle, twist it away from you (clockwise) as before, then bring it down in front of the other bundle, which now becomes the top bundle. Take this new top bundle and repeat the twisting and bringing down. Keep repeating.

8. When you feel one bundle thinning, add in more material: lay in a new stem on the bottom bundle (as shown), then twist the top bundle as usual. Add small amounts of material frequently so your cordage has a consistent thickness.

128 | **Wild Basketry**

9. Added-in fibres leave a tail, which you can trim away at the end.

10. To finish, tie a knot in the end.

Bramble Cordage

Fibres are extracted from the bramble bast

Bramble (blackberry) grows commonly in woodland, hedges and scrub. It is native to temperate Europe and naturalised in North America and Australasia. Bramble has long, thorny and arching stems and can grow up to two metres (80 inches) or more high. Small pink and white flowers mature into the dark purple blackberries that are known so well.

You will need:
- One or two stems 1m (39in) long, diameter 8mm (0.3in)
- Secateurs
- Sturdy gloves
- Small craft knife (lockable or fixed blade)
- Small round stone
- Thick, sharp needle

Harvesting
Harvest in early summer.

1. Use secateurs to cut one or two new shoots that are approximately 1m (3ft) in length and 8mm (0.3in) in diameter, without side shoots.

2. Wearing tough gloves, run your hand up and down the bramble stems to remove thorns and leaves.

Tip
If you're scraping away white fibres, you're scraping too hard and deep.

3. Use the back of your knife blade to gently scrape away the very thin epidermis on the stem (the green 'skin'). Your knife must have a fixed or lockable blade, for safety.

4. Firmly tap the scraped stem with your stone, all the way along. You'll see the fibres start to separate.

5. Pull these fibres off the stem and keep them. Discard the rest.

PROJECTS

6. Split these fibres into thin strands by inserting your needle then drawing it along, first in one direction then the other.

7. Make the strands as thin as you possibly can. You can store these until you're ready to use them.

8. Take a small bundle of split fibres (between three and seven strands). Allow the ends to be staggered; don't line them up. At roughly the midpoint, hold the bundle between your left thumb and index finger. With your right hand, twist the bundle away from you for about 5cm (2in).

Tip
Make the twist by pulling the pad of your thumb towards you while holding the fibres between that thumb and index finger. Dampen your thumb and fingers when needed.

Wild Basketry

9. Bring your hands together and the twisted length will naturally kink to make a small loop, as shown. If it doesn't kink, your twist needs to be a little tighter.

10. Hold the small loop with your left hand so that you have two bundles sticking out to the right. With your right hand, take the top bundle, twist it away from you (clockwise) as before, then bring it down in front of the other bundle, which now becomes the top bundle. Take this new top bundle and repeat the twisting and bringing down. Keep repeating.

11. When you feel one bundle thinning, add in more material: lay in new fibres on the bottom bundle (as shown), then twist the top bundle as usual. Add small amounts of fibre frequently so your cordage has a consistent thickness.

12. Added-in fibres leave a tail, which you can trim away at the end. To finish, tie a knot in the end.

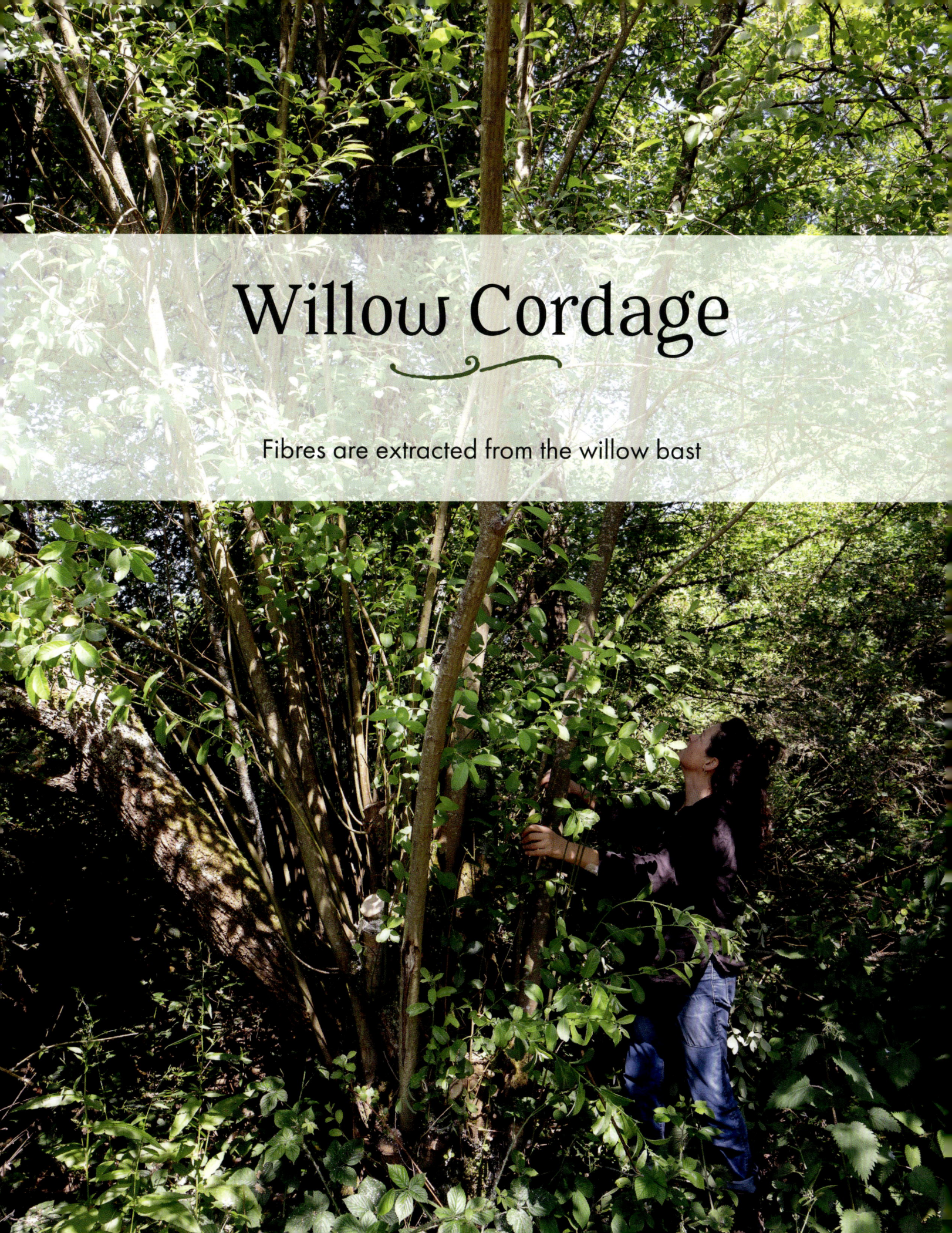

Willow Cordage

Fibres are extracted from the willow bast

There are many species of willow, found primarily on moist soils in cold and temperate regions. They grow as deciduous trees and shrubs, and are among the earliest woody plants to leaf out in spring and the last to drop their leaves in autumn. Willow roots are remarkable for their toughness and tenacity, and they also readily sprout from aerial parts of the plant.

Most willows are suitable for cordage; this project shows goat willow (*Salix caprea*), as a lot grows in my area.

You will need:
- One willow branch 75cm long (29.5in), diameter approx. 3cm (1in)
- Small handsaw
- Small craft knife (lockable or fixed blade)
- Scissors

Harvesting and Preparation
Harvest in spring when the sap is well risen and leaves have opened, selecting a small branch from a pollarded or coppiced tree. Sometimes this type of growth occurs naturally when a tree is felled by a storm. Choose a reasonably straight branch that's free from bark damage with a healthy number of leaves.

1. Saw at the base of the branch with a supporting hand holding it, as shown. Make sure that you can easily get close to the branch, there's space for it to come down safely when you saw and no people or animals are close by. Leave a smooth cut edge to protect the health of the tree.

Making
2. Scrape off the green epidermis (outer 'skin') with either the back of the saw (as shown) or the back of your knife blade (your knife must have a fixed or lockable blade for safety). Do not scrape away the white fibres.

3. Carefully score a straight line down the length with your knife, holding the branch as shown and resting the bottom of the branch on your workbench. Press lightly with your knife so that you stay in control of the blade.

4. Peel away the inner bark. Avoid splitting it as much as possible.

5. Gently flatten the inner bark and use scissors to cut long, even, thin strips, no more than 2mm (0.8in) wide.

6. Take three strips – don't line up the ends but let them be staggered. At roughly the midpoint, hold the bundle between your left thumb and index finger. With your right hand, twist the bundle away from you for about 5cm (2in). Use material that is only just damp enough to manipulate to avoid the cordage drying with gaps in it.

Wild Basketry

7. Bring your hands together and the twisted length will naturally kink to make a small loop. If it doesn't kink, your twist needs to be a little tighter.

8. Hold the small loop with your left hand so you have two bundles sticking out to the right. Twist the top bundle away from you (clockwise). Bring it down in front of the other bundle, which now becomes the top bundle. Take this new top bundle and keep repeating the twisting and bringing down.

9. When you feel one bundle thinning, add in more material: lay in new fibres on the bottom bundle then twist the top bundle as usual. Add small amounts of fibre frequently so your cordage has a consistent thickness. Dampen your willow strips if they start feeling stiff, by dipping them very briefly in water.

10. Added-in fibres leave a tail, which you can trim away at the end. To finish, tie a knot in the end.

PROJECT 4
Phormium
Phormium spp.

Phormium is an evergreen perennial plant native to New Zealand and Norfolk Island, Australia and its Māori name is 'Wharariki'. Europeans, who were familiar with flax fibres, named it as New Zealand flax but it's actually related to the daylily, hemerocallis.

Phormium grows as a clump of long, sword-shaped leaves up to two metres (80 inches) long, and its dramatic yellow or red flowers grow on tall shoots. It can protect an area from soil erosion as it prefers wetter conditions with good drainage and doesn't require much soil depth. There are many cultivars, with variegated and coloured leaves, grown as ornamental plants for their architectural form. Any phormium leaf will work for this project, whatever colour it is.

↑Tūī feeding on *Phormium tenax*

The Phormium Community

A phormium bush can support a large community of animals. Native birds that feed on the nectar of the flower include the tūī, korimako (bellbirds), tīeke (saddlebacks), hihi (stitchbirds), kākā, kākāriki (parrots) and tauhou (white eyes). Geckos, pekapeka (lesser short-tailed bats), and several types of insects also feed on the nectar.

Pūpū harakeke (flax snails) – a rare land snail living only in the far north of New Zealand – shelter under phormium bushes feeding on fallen leaves from native broadleaf trees. The flax looper caterpillar (*Orthoclydon praefectata*), native to New Zealand, feeds on the underside of the leaves, leaving a 'window' of the leaf cuticle; the flax notcher moth (*Ichneutica steropastis*) leaves notches at the edges of young leaves. Phormium seed is also a food source for pārera (grey duck).

For the Māori people of New Zealand, phormium is an important material and cultural plant. Baskets, containers and mats are woven from it and the fibres (muka) are extracted by scraping and pounding, then twisted, plaited and woven. Items such as fishing traps and nets, footwear, cords and ropes are made from these strong fibres.

Traditionally, special plants are carefully tended in a plantation, with clear guidelines about when and how to harvest the leaves. The central shoot (rito) was thought to be the baby and the leaves either side of it were its parents. Only the leaves on the outside, the grandparents (tupuna), are cut so as to avoid weakening the plant.

Phormium Net Bag

This project uses a looping technique

PROJECTS

This project uses a cording and looping technique to make a net bag suitable for a flask or bottle. Only attempt to create it if you've already made at least two metres of good strong cordage (see Phormium Cordage on page 120).

You will need:
- Four or five phormium leaves
- Secateurs
- Large sharp needle
- Heckling comb (optional)
- String
- Tape
- Small scissors
- Flask/bottle (7cm/2.75in diameter at base)

Harvesting
Harvest at any time of year.

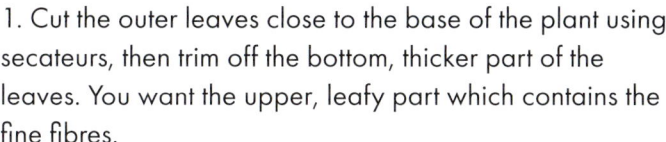

1. Cut the outer leaves close to the base of the plant using secateurs, then trim off the bottom, thicker part of the leaves. You want the upper, leafy part which contains the fine fibres.

Wild Basketry | 143

Preparation

2. The leaves have a raised rib running down the centre. Halfway along, pierce the leaf with your needle next to the rib and split the leaf by drawing the needle along, first in one direction then in the other.

3. Repeat on the other side of the rib. Discard the rib.

4. Use the needle in the same way to split the leaf into very thin strips of fibre, as narrow as you can possibly make them. Use your thumb to scrape away the green material, revealing the pale fibres. This splitting and scraping process can also be done with a heckling comb, if you have one, by repeatedly pulling the leaf across the sharp points of the comb.

Making

5. This starts differently from the cordage in Project 3. Take two small bundles of fibres of two or three strands each. Holding them together in the middle with your left hand, with an upper and lower bundle, make 3cm (1.1in) cordage. This should be half the thickness of the cordage that you want to end up with.

6. Bring both the loose ends together to form an arch, as shown.

7. Pair each loose end with one from the other bundle, so that they swap partners. Continue cording to create a secure loop about 2.5cm (1in) diameter. Extend your cordage to an arm's length to start the looping.

8. Holding the small loop steady, poke the other end (the working end) into it and then out from under, towards you, as shown. Pull it through until it creates a loop the same size as the existing loop.

Tip
Dampen your right-hand finger and thumb pads to help with twisting the fibres.

9. Work anticlockwise, making five more loops around the initial loop to create a six-petalled flower. This flower should be the same diameter as your flask.

10. Secure this looped flower to the base of your flask tightly with string (I slipped a leaf between, just to show this more clearly). Tape the string top and bottom to keep it steady.

11. Extend your cordage by another arm's length. Continue looping anticlockwise, going into the first petal and then into each subsequent loop as you work round in a spiral so that you start coming up the sides of your flask. Keep the loops the same size so that it all fits snugly on your flask. Carry on looping, extending the cordage as needed.

Tip
Fill the flask with water as its weight will make it more steady. Work with the flask on your lap with its top pointing towards you.

12. The looping will stretch when you're carrying the bag so stop looping well before the top, where your flask narrows. On the last loop, make an extra small loop into it, pulling it tight to create a half hitch. This secures the looping.

Finishing
13. Thread the working end in and out of each top loop all the way round.

14. Make another half hitch.

Tip
Before you make the final half hitches, measure the strap against your body to make sure it's the length you want.

15. For a shoulder strap, make sure your cordage is approximately 2.5m (98in) long. Take the working end across to the other side of your flask and thread through the top loop. Bring it back to the side where the half hitches are and make two more half hitches to secure the end of your cordage. Finally, tie a knot in the end of your working end.

Development
Experiment with different fibres and thicknesses of cordage.

→ Looped bags made of English rush

PROJECT 5

Grass

Poaceae spp.

Grasses are widespread across the world; in fact, grasslands cover 30 per cent of the total land area of Earth. There are approximately 10,000 species of grass, which make up one-third of all flowering plants on our planet.

The Grassland Community

Butterflies that you'll find in grasslands include: chequered skipper, meadow brown, green hairstreak, grizzled skipper, Essex skipper, gatekeeper, ringlet, small heath, small skipper, Scotch argus, marbled white and speckled wood.

Grasslands and meadows produce abundant seeds, nectar and pollen and provide an important habitat for invertebrates, which in turn are a key food source for many birds. Red-tailed mason bees (their unique building techniques are described on page 32) live on chalk and limestone grasslands. Small mammals that live among grasses are mice, harvest mice, voles and shrews. Adders live on heathlands and grass snakes can be found on grasslands where there's water nearby.

Birds that depend on grassland habitats include skylarks and meadow pipits, who both nest on the ground. Seed-rich grasslands provide important food for overwintering grain-eating birds, such as yellowhammers and reed buntings. Falcons and buzzards use grasslands to hunt and bats feed on insects that are active at dusk and at night in open grassland.

Barn owls rely on species-rich meadows, which are a haven for small mammals – food for the owls. Over a year, a breeding pair of barn owls needs roughly 4,000 prey items. They are unable to digest the fur and bone of their prey, which they usually swallow whole. The indigestible parts are regurgitated as an owl pellet. After feeding, it takes the owl six hours or more to produce a pellet, and after each night's hunting an owl regurgitates one or two pellets. Barn owl pellets are typically about the size of a large thumb. They are black when fresh, dark grey when dry. Pellets often contain the remains of four or five small mammals, and if you dissect the pellet it can tell you exactly what an owl has eaten. Pellets often accumulate at roosting or nesting sites, where owls can hide away and shelter from the weather. Barn owls are a protected species and it is illegal to disturb them while they're breeding.

The harvest mouse (*Micromys minutus*) is the 'smallest tiny mouse'. It lives among tall grasses, reeds and cereal crops. It builds its nest about half a metre (20 inches) above the ground using carefully woven grass, lined with thistledown and chewed grass. The nest is an almost perfect sphere, about the size of a cricket ball and tightly anchored to the surrounding stems. Adults are the length of your thumb and weigh less than 10g. They have acute hearing, which allows them to detect the slightest rustle from up to seven metres (23 feet) away, which is equivalent

↓ Marbled white butterflies on meadow plants

↓ Barn owl over grassland

↓ Harvest mouse nest in tall grass

to a human hearing a twig snap 300 metres (1,000 feet) away. Their prehensile tail grips stems like a fifth limb so that they can climb nimbly in search of insects and grass or cereal seeds. They still cling on in agricultural fields, grassy hedgerows, bramble patches and reedbeds, but seeing one in the wild is rare. The harvest mouse is now listed as a priority species of conservation concern.

Brown hares are most common in a mosaic of arable fields, grasslands and hedgerows, grazing on vegetation and the bark of young trees and bushes. They don't dig burrows, but shelter in 'forms', which are shallow depressions in the grass. When disturbed, they can be seen bounding across the fields, using their powerful hind legs to propel them forwards, often in a zigzag pattern.

The grass family is widely valued around the world by people for making a huge array of different kinds of objects. Straw from cereal crops (rice, wheat, oats, rye and barley) is traditionally stitched, twisted and plaited into corn dollies, harvest knots, protective talismans or charms, hats, costumes, rain capes, mats, rope, thatch, containers for domestic fowl, animal tethers, bee skeps and grain stores. Lipwork is the name given to coiled and stitched straw or grass baskets and furniture, as a widespread tradition, wherever these materials grow or are cultivated.

Bamboo is the largest member of the grass family – the fastest-growing plant in the world. Species are found in diverse climates, from cold mountains to hot tropical regions, mainly in India, Indonesia, China, Japan, Africa and Australia. It's native to temperate and tropical zones of every continent, except Europe and Antarctica. It's historically used in every aspect of daily life, for building construction, in fencing, traps, tools, furniture, basketry, textiles, paper, musical instruments, weapons and water pipes.

Queshuachaca is a Peruvian grass bridge, and a feat of engineering. Rope made from fragile grass material is formed into a bridge with a span of 36 metres (118 feet) across a river canyon. It's rebuilt annually by the community and creates social regeneration and reinforcement. Japanese Shinto straw rope, shimenawa, is used at shrines to demarcate sacred spaces. There is also the extraordinary work of Angus McPhee, a Scottish man who made outsize clothing from looped grass cordage in the twentieth century.

Lidded Grass Basket

This project uses the coiling technique

You will need:

- Five handfuls of long-stemmed grass, approx. 250g in weight
- Small craft knife
- Watering can
- Hessian or old towels
- Twine
- Large sharp needle
- Scissors
- Secateurs
- Short length of wood
- Drill

Harvesting

Harvest in August or September. The species of grass to cut isn't important; what matters is its stems – you want grass with long, thin stems for this basket. Many grasses will be suitable if left uncut, and good places to look are unmown verges and field margins. Cut your grass once the seeds have fallen – in the British Isles this is generally from August onwards.

1. Cut stems close to the base of the plant and lay out to dry for a couple of weeks in a warm, airy place. Tie in a bundle and store in a dry place until you're ready to use them.

Preparation

2. The night before, drench the grasses in water (I use a watering can), then wrap them in a large piece of hessian (old towels will do).

Making the Base

3. Take some grass stems to make a bundle with a diameter of approximately 12mm (0.5in). Line up the butts (the cut ends) and tie a length of twine to the end of the bundle, knotting it tightly.

4. Wrap the twine tightly around the bundle in an anticlockwise direction, as shown, for 10.5cm (4.1in).

5. Thread the needle onto the long end of your twine. Fold the tip ends of the grasses across to the left and insert the needle, as shown. Pull the needle to the back and out, making the stitch tight.

6. Continue stitching, inserting the needle in the top of the bundle below, slightly to the right of each stitch.

7. Keep the bundle of grass (the core) at a uniform thickness, which means adding new grass stems every two or three stitches. To do this, poke in three or four butt ends (as shown), making sure they go deeply into the centre of the core. Carry on stitching.

8. When you run out of twine, knot in a new length, making your knot close to the basket.

9. As the size of the base increases, you'll need to add an extra stitch now and then to keep the size of the space between stitches consistent. To do this, just make another stitch when the space feels too big – ideally inserting the needle into the same place as the previous stitch – to create a V.

Shaping the Base

10. When the base is approximately 18 × 10cm (7 × 4in), start making the side of the basket. To do this, lift the core away from you slightly and then stitch it in place as before. Continue stitching and adding in new grasses until the sides of your basket reach a height of 6cm (2.3in).

Finishing the Base

11. Do a couple of extra stitches and then insert the needle in and out of a couple of rows below to secure the twine. Snip the end of the twine, then snip the grass stems off.

156 | **Wild Basketry**

Making the Lid

12. Follow previous Steps 3–9 to make an oval disc that sits on top of your basket, closely matched in size. Finish the stitching as in Step 11.

Tip
To get a snug-fitting lid, make sure the lip is the right distance from the edge so that it will sit just inside the basket.

13. On the side that you want to be the inside of the lid, stitch on a new coil all the way round, just inside from the edge. This creates a lip. The stitches on the first round go through to the other side of the lid and back again each time.

14. For the second round of the coil, stitch in the same way you stitched the basket. Finish off the stitching as before.

Making the Handle

15. Find a short length of wood. I chose a piece of honeysuckle, cut it to length with secateurs, and then scraped off the outer bark. Drill a hole at each end.

16. Make a couple of stitches through the holes to secure the handles. Finish off with a knot on the underside of the lid.

Development

Use other pliable stems or leaves such as iris, crocosmia, daffodil or daylily. Experiment with different twines for stitching.

PROJECT 6

Reed Mace
Typha latifolia

Reed mace – also known as cattail or bulrush – is native to Eurasia, North and South America and Africa. It grows in shallow fresh water to 1.5–3m (59–118in) tall, and is often found in ditches, ponds and swamps. Its leaves are 10–20mm (0.4–0.8in) wide and smooth with a blueish hue. The brown cigar-shaped seed head is unmistakeable if present, and when it goes to seed it produces very fine fluff. It's considered an invasive species. Lesser reed mace (*Typha angustifolia*) is similar but with narrower leaves.

Yellow flag iris (*Iris pseudacorus*) is a lookalike plant, which tends to grow less tall than reed mace. Its leaves are emerald green with a longitudinal ribbed texture, and bright yellow flowers appear between May and August. The base of the leaf bundles are oval in cross-section; those of reed mace are round.

↓ Water rail

The Reed Mace Community

The bulrush wainscot moth (*Nonagria typhae*) is found exclusively on Typha species and is nationally rare. It is a large, distinctive species with a wingspan of up to 54mm (2.1in). The larvae feed on the stems of reed mace and lesser reed mace and pupate inside the stem until they fly in August. Other wainscot moths who feed on bulrush are Webb's wainscot (*Globia sparganii*), rush wainscot (*Globia algae*) and also bulrush cosmet (*Limnaecia phragmitella*), whose larvae feed on the seed heads in winter.

The ecosystem that reed mace grows in supports many aquatic insects: mayflies and dragonflies throng the messy and vegetative margins of lakes and ponds; warm shallow waters are good for invertebrates. Bulrush bugs (*Chilacis typhae*) are small beetles who rely on reed mace. The adults can be seen pairing any time between spring and autumn, often on the seed heads, and they frequently overwinter inside the seed heads. At times they can be very numerous, with over 1,000 individuals found in a single seed head.

Reed mace acts as cover for wildlife: for wading birds such as snipes and water rails. Reed warblers and bearded tits may also be found in this habitat, especially where common reed (*Phragmites*) is also growing.

Water voles – endangered in the UK – live in burrows on the banks of rivers, streams, ponds and ditches, preferring more open wetland habitats away from tree cover. They are expert swimmers and divers and mainly eat grass and other vegetation near the water, but they will also consume fruits, bulbs, twigs, buds and roots when they have the chance. Shrews, frogs, newts and toads can be found in non-flowing water when breeding.

Bats feed over water, on insects that are active at dusk and at night. Hedgerows, streams and trees are important flight paths and foraging opportunities for bats.

Parts of the plant are edible for humans: the rhizomes can be cooked – skin removed – and are quite starchy. The young leaf bases can be eaten raw or cooked. The young flower spikes and the sprouts at the end of the rootstocks are also edible. If you're eating any part of the plant, it's important to make sure the water it's growing in isn't polluted.

There's a long, widespread tradition of weaving and constructing with the leaves and stems of reeds and rushes. The Marsh Arabs of Southern Iraq create incredible structures with ihdri reed. These are tied in tight bundles – the thicker ends of the reed at the base of the bundle – and made into parabolic arches to construct small dwellings up to large meeting halls, over 15 metres (49 feet) in length. At Lake Titicaca in Bolivia, rush (*Schoenoplectus* spp.) is made into boats and floating huts.

↓ Water vole

Reed Mace Basket

This project uses a twining technique

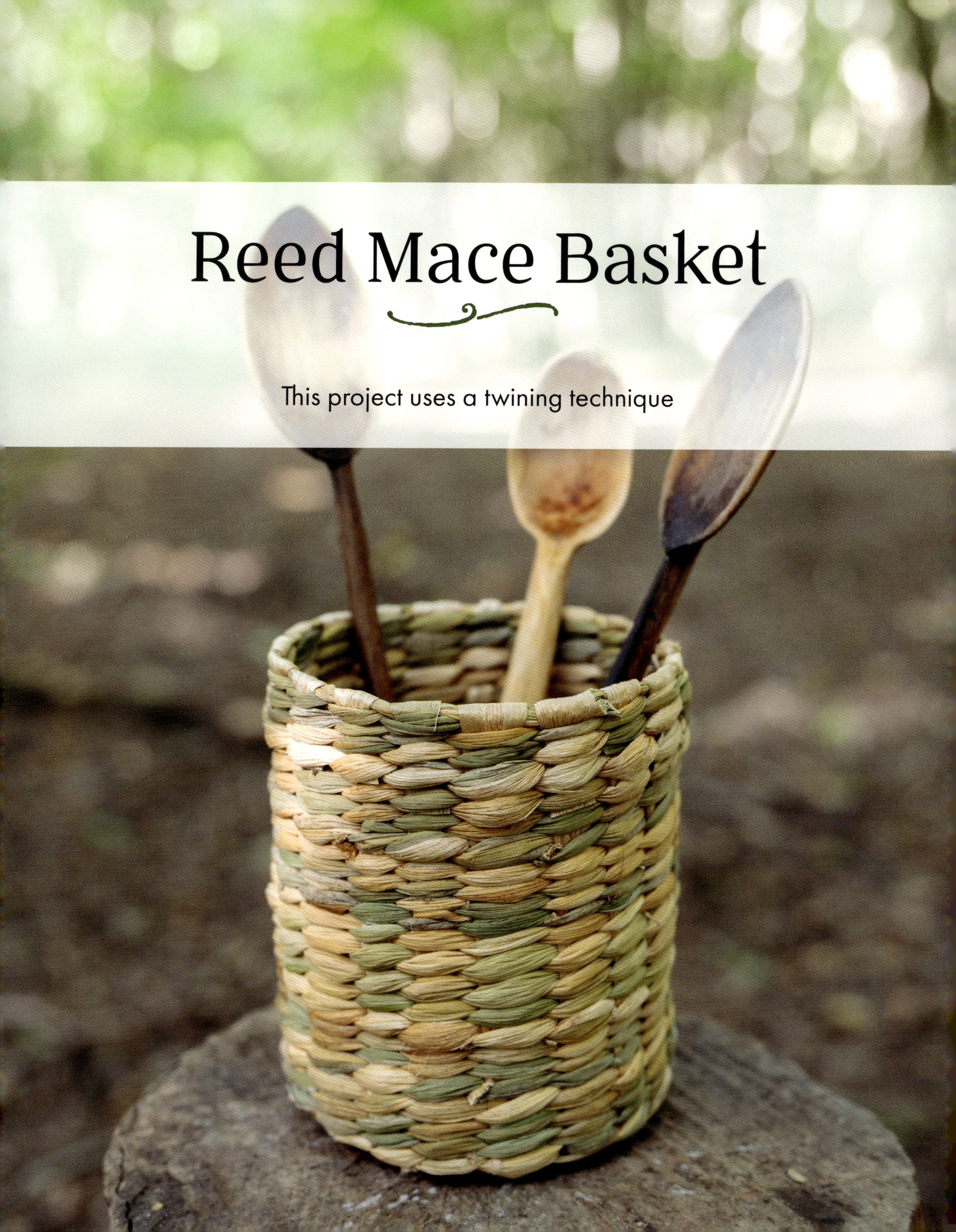

You will need:
- About twelve reed mace leaves (equivalent to three plants)
- Small craft knife
- Watering can
- Hessian or old towels
- String
- Tape
- Scissors
- A cylindrical object to be your mould. I've used a glass storage jar, height 15cm (6in), diameter 10cm (4in)

Harvesting

Harvest in late August or September; earlier harvesting risks disturbing wainscot moths that feed on (and pupate inside) the stems of the plant. Where the moth larvae are active, you can usually see holes of approximately 6mm (0.2in) diameter in the lower part of the stem. If you see this, do not cut that plant, as the larva or pupa may still be inside.

PROJECTS

1. Cut as close to the base of the plant as you can, which may be below the water line. Reed mace often grows in deep mud, so take care when cutting.

2. Do not cut plants that have a seed head – the brown, velvety cigar shape on top.

3. Separate the leaves.

4. Lay the leaves out in a dry, airy environment for 2–3 weeks. Once dry, tie them in a bundle and store in a dry place, away from direct sunlight or heat, until you're ready to use them. If you're in a warm, dry climate you can dry the plants without separating the leaves.

Wild Basketry | 165

Preparation

5. The night before, drench your reed mace in water (I use a watering can) and wrap it in a large piece of hessian (old towels will do). Once dampened, you can gently fold the bundle in half, as shown.

6. The next day, cut the bottom, thicker ends (butts) of 10 leaves to twice the height of your intended basket plus the diameter of your mould, adding an extra 32cm (12.5in) for the border (for this basket (13cm (5.1in) high), I cut 70cm (27.5in) lengths). These are the 10 stakes of your basket.

Making

7. The thinner ends of the leaves (tips) will be your weavers; set these aside. Take your stakes, measure for the midpoint and tie them very tightly together with string.

8. Fan out the stakes.

9. From your bundle of leaf tip ends, select a nice long one. Find the point that is one-third of the way along its length and place it behind two of the fanned-out stakes so that the two ends come to the front, as shown. These two ends are your weavers.

10. The left-hand weaver moves across in front of two stakes...

11. ...Then it goes behind two stakes and back to the front. You have completed one stroke of the weave. This is the weave used for the whole basket and it's called 'pairing'.

12. Continue around all the stakes this way, always moving the left-hand weaver first: going in front of two stakes, behind two stakes and back to the front each time. Go around twice like this.

13. On the third round, start weaving around the stakes singly, rather than in twos.

14. Carry on weaving until your weavers start to run out.

Adding a Weaver

15. Add in a new weaver when the right-hand one is 8cm (3.1in) long. Slide its tip end behind the current stake so it lays alongside the left-hand weaver by 8cm (3.1in). Now on each side you will have a shorter tip end alongside a longer weaver. Treat the two on each side as one and double them up to weave.

16. Continue weaving as before, then when the tips become too short to keep including, leave them behind, as shown. You'll trim them off later.

17. Weave until you have a disc that is the same size as the base of your mould. Tie this disc tightly onto your mould with two lengths of string, crossing at the bottom, as shown.

18. Tape the string to the sides of your mould.

19. On your lap, continue weaving as before, going up the sides of your mould. Add in new weavers when needed.

20. Stop weaving when you get to within 8cm (3.1in) of the top of your mould or when your stakes are 12cm (4.7in) long – whichever comes first.

> **Tip**
> Depending on your speed and the ambient temperature, your material may dry out and become stiff or brittle. Spray the stakes and working weavers (not the woven part) with water and wrap them in hessian (or a towel) for 30 minutes.

The Border

21. Now when you weave, fold down each stake to the rim of your mould before the left-hand weaver passes across in front of it, then complete the stroke as before.

22. Continue all the way around, adding in weavers when needed so that all the stakes are looped.

23. Weave another three rounds, making sure you end up with one long weaver (long enough to wrap around the circumference of your mould). Trim the other weaver, as shown.

24. Thread the short weaver through two loops, then thread the long weaver through each loop all the way round. Pull it snug.

25. Gently but firmly pull down the stakes to close the loops and secure the threaded weavers.

Finishing

26. Trim the stakes and any sticking-out bits with a sharp pair of scissors. Cut the string and take out the mould.

Development
Experiment with using other long, flexible leaves such as daylily, iris and juncus.

Tip
When trimming, gently pull the reed mace away so it stretches slightly; trim up close to the basket so that when you cut, the cut end more or less disappears into the weave.

Foraging Wild Plants: The Law

Below are guidelines to UK law on foraging. Be sure to check localised laws and regulations specific to your region or host country.

In the UK, the right to forage has been enshrined in British law since at least the thirteenth century. Unlike land, plants are common goods, not 'property'. It's always best to forage where there are clear rights of access and with the landowner's permission. The '4 F' rule is that you can pick flowers, fungi, fruit and foliage from anywhere you have legal access to.

More specifically, when gathering any wild plants for basketmaking, be aware of these guidelines:

- Seek permission from the landowner before accessing private land.
- Only pick what you will use.
- Only take from plentiful populations, and then take no more than 50 per cent.
- Uprooting any plant is illegal unless you have the landowner's permission.
- Some plants are specifically protected by law and cannot be picked or disturbed unless you have the appropriate licence.
- On protected areas, such as National Nature Reserves and Sites of Special Scientific Interest, there may be a ban on picking any vegetation.

UK Wildlife and Countryside Act 1981:
legislation.gov.uk/ukpga/1981/69

Land Reform (Scotland) Act 2003:
legislation.gov.uk/asp/2003/2/contents

Botanical Society of Britain & Ireland:
bsbi.org

Author teaching bramble baskets in Sussex, UK ➜

Bibliography

Barber, E., *Women's Work: The First 2,000 Years*: Norton, 1995

Bate, J. (ed.), *Selected Poetry of John Clare*: Faber & Faber, 2004

Berry, W., *The Collected Poems*: North Point Press, 2005

Bell, J. A., *Basketry: Making Human Nature*: Sainsbury Centre for Visual Arts, 2011

Bichard, M., *Baskets in Europe*: Fyfield Wick Editions, 2008

Bolton, L., *Baskets and Belonging: Indigenous Australian Histories*: British Museum, 2011

Bunn, S. and Mitchell, V. (eds), *The Material Culture of Basketry*: Bloomsbury, 2021

Drury, C., *Chris Drury: Silent Spaces*: Thames & Hudson, 1998

Friedman, T. and Goldsworthy, A., *Hand to Earth: Andy Goldsworthy: Sculpture 1976–1990*: Thames & Hudson, 2006

Hansell, M., *Built by Animals: The Natural History of Animal Architecture*: Oxford University Press, 2007

Hayes, N., *The Book of Trespass*: Bloomsbury, 2020

Heslop, T. A. and Anderson, H. (eds), *Basketry and Beyond: Constructing Cultures*: SRU UEA, 2020

Hogan, J., *Basketmaking in Ireland*: Wordwell, 2021

Kimmerer, R. W., *Braiding Sweetgrass: Indigenous Wisdom, Scientific Knowledge, and the Teachings of Plants*: Milkweed Editions, 2013

Marshall Thomas, E., *The Old Way: A Story of the First People*: Farrar Straus & Giroux, 2006

O'Dowd, A., *Straw, Hay & Rushes in Irish Folk Tradition*: Irish Academic Press, 2015

Sentance, B., *Basketry: A World Guide to Traditional Techniques*: Thames & Hudson, 2007

Soffer, O., Adovasio, J. and Hyland, D., *The 'Venus' Figurines: Textiles, Basketry, Gender and Status in the Upper Palaeolithic*. Current Anthropology 41(4) 511:537, 2007

Tree, I., *Wilding: The Return of Nature to a British Farm*: Pan Macmillan, 2018

Walpole, L., *Kishies and Cuddies, A Guide to the Traditional Basketry of Shetland*: Walpole Press, 2024

Resources

Barn Owl Trust
www.barnowltrust.org.uk

British Trust for Ornithology
www.bto.org

Butterfly Conservation
butterfly-conservation.org

Heritage Crafts Association:
heritagecrafts.org.uk

How Wolves Change Rivers (Yellowstone National Park, USA): **youtube.com/watch?v=W88Sact1kws**

Traditional Basketry Project:
basketmakersassociation.org.uk/traditional-basketry-project

UK Butterflies
www.ukbutterflies.co.uk

UK Moths
ukmoths.org.uk

The Wildlife Trusts
www.wildlifetrusts.org

The Woodland Trust
www.woodlandtrust.org.uk

Woven Communities Project (the Scottish Basketmakers Circle and Dr Stephanie Bunn): **wovencommunities.org**

Photo credits

All photos copyright of the author unless otherwise stated.

p12, 23 (both), 62, 65 (both), 66, 82: Bethany Hobbs, **beehobbs.co.uk**

p29: Jeanne K Simmons

p34: Caroline Dear

p41 (bottom): René de Saint-Périer

p42 (top): Bjørn Christian Tørrissen

p42 (bottom): Historic Images/Alamy Stock Photo

p48: Chris Drury

p80: Martin Hill and Philippa Jones

p56: Lorna Singleton, **lornasingleton.co.uk**. Photo courtesy Tiree Dawson/Random Chair Ltd

pp57, 60 (top right): Dominic Parrette, **sussexwillow.co.uk**

p58: Lewis Goldwater, **turnham-green-wood.co.uk**

p59: Jo Hammond (**@twignstuff**). Photo courtesy The Merchants Table

p60 (top left): Rachael Frost (**@thecrafty_beggars**)

p60 (bottom): John Williamson, **dartmoorwoodcraft.co.uk**. Photo courtesy Suzy Bennett

p86: Valentyn Volkov

p87: Wim Verhagen

p88: Ian Newell

p103: Fotowada

p104: JMrocek

p140: ClaudineVM

p141: Wirestock

p152 (left): Heather Wilde

p152 (right): Michel Viard

p161: Helen Davies

p162: Stacy Woolhouse

p176: © Jody Daunton

With thanks to Samuel Green, Megan West and Natasa Leoni **natasaleoni.com**

Permissions

p8: Le Guin, U. K., *The Carrier Bag Theory of Fiction*: Ignota, 2019

pp9, 14, 74, 76, 78: © Robin Wall Kimmerer, *Braiding Sweetgrass: Indigenous Wisdom, Scientific Knowledge, and the Teachings of Plants* (Penguin, 2013)

p20: © Caroline Dear from Bunn, S. and Mitchell, V. (eds), *The Material Culture of Basketry* (Bloomsbury Visual Arts, 2021)

p27: 'Basket' by Kay Syrad (2023), **kaysyrad.co.uk**. Reproduced with permission

Acknowledgements

Although one person, one pair of hands weaves a basket, there are many threads of life and many conditions that help bring it, finally, into being. So it is with writing a book.

To the sweet-smelling hayfields and grasslands that my bare feet have known I'm thankful. For the trees I have rested and dreamt beneath: the Oxfordshire beeches, Devon oaks and Sussex hornbeams. It was bramble that first ignited my curiosity about weaving baskets from the plant kin around me, all of whom have been inspiring and forthright teachers since.

For the people, thanks to my parents who encouraged my creativity and love of the living world from a young age. In writing this book, particular thanks to Clare Martelli and Natasha Collin at Bloomsbury. Thank you Patricia van den Akker for your support. Thanks also to Dr Hilary Leighton for the generous foreword, Kay Syrad for the basket poem, and Sam Green for your stalwart contribution and friendship. Thanks are also due to Michael Blencowe and Mary Butcher for their respective expertise. Many other people – friends, family and colleagues – have given their time to helping and encouraging me with this book. Many more have helped in one way or another to shape the ideas within it. I have been fortunate to meet generous and gifted teachers and guides through the years, and people who have been catalysts, inspirations and enablers. There are too many to name individually, but it's true that I wouldn't be here without you, and I am thankful to each one of you.

Thanks to the ESAMP team, Tristan Bareham, Christabel Shelley, Ian Dunford and the late Piers Chandler, who generously opened my eyes with life-changing results. Gratitude to the basketry tutors at City Lit from whom I first learnt invaluable fundamentals and applications of basketry techniques and who encouraged me: Mary Butcher, Shuna Rendel, John Page, Polly Pollock. Thanks also to Iain Parkinson for creative opportunities.

I'm grateful to all the people who have come to learn with me, and in doing so have taught me a great deal. Special thanks to Amanda Norman and family for generously making so much possible, and for the laughs.